First Hardcover Edition: November 2003

ABOUT THE BOOK:

Finally, here is a book that deals bluntly and realistically with academic achievement and career accomplishments. One common denominator of successful individuals is that they know how to apply, execute and translate lessons learned in class or on the job to everyday life. In this concise book, you will learn how to bring substantial accomplishments into your life - - personally, professionally, financially and spiritually. Read it, digest it, but most importantly, act on it! You will then feel uplifted, empowered and determined to achieve significant, fulfilling results. Anyone who wants to stimulate the seeds of greatness within his or her life will find this book invaluable.

STRAIGHT TALK

STIMULATING IDEAS FOR TRUE ACADEMIC DEVELOPMENT

LEARN, THINK AND ACT TO ACCOMPLISH AND ACHIEVE

written by

HARLYNN LAVANCE HAMMONDS

The one book to read on how to
MAXIMIZE YOUR POTENTIAL

Published by

InSpire Me Publishing
P.O. Box 8351, Reston, VA 20195

ISBN: 1-4140-0621-7 (e-book)
ISBN: 1-4140-0622-5 (Paperback)
ISBN: 1-4140-0623-3 (Dust Jacket)

Library of Congress Control Number: 2003098160

This book is printed on acid free paper.

Printed in the United States of America
Bloomington, IN

1stBooks – rev. 04/20/04

Turn the pages of this book
and this is what you will find!

- **Applied knowledge, combined with educational goals and priorities,** to stimulate a successful academic journey. **Chapter 1.**

- **Emerging synergies** to invest our minds, abilities, talents and time to reach an abundant return. **Chapter 8.**

- **Academic preparation and personal career development principles** to propel your career advancement. **Chapter 4.**

- **Time management principles** to accomplish more in less time with consistency of effort. **Chapter 6.**

- **Marketing strategies** to finding and keeping a career building position and becoming an asset to every organization. **Chapter 5.**

- **Get and stay motivated** to maintain energy and momentum to achieve success in any field or endeavor. **Chapter 3.**

- **Quality thoughts** to keep you focused, organized and inspired on your life vision, goals, objectives and unlimited potential. **Chapter 2.**

- **Cash and personal asset management principles** to strengthen your long-term financial stability. **Chapter 7.**

- **Bible verses** to enhance your spiritual journey and understanding. **Appendixes 1 through 8.**

TABLE OF CONTENTS

ACKNOWLEDGEMENTS

This book is dedicated to my loving parents: the late Herbert Hammonds (deceased) and Robertine Hammonds (step-mother), Edward Sears (deceased) and Ramona Brazil Sears (mother). We truly are "ONE BIG" happy family. I love you for giving me the love, guidance and incentive to work hard at my goals with fierce determination and persistence.

A definite thanks is extended to Alison Bethel, Washington Bureau Chief for the Detroit News. She worked with me to transform my final manuscript to produce an even better book than I had originally envisioned.

I thank Rachelle Gould-Harris for interpreting my hopelessly inept drawings into engaging illustrations; she has a gift for making order out of chaos.

Special mention is made of Ruby Higgins, Vice President of Student Affairs at Grambling State University and other deserving faculty members who have influenced and touched my life. A heartfelt thank you is extended to others in my network of family and friends.

It goes without saying, I dedicate this book to my heavenly Father, to whom I owe the most, for inspiring me to search within and express every written thought. My business aspirations have now taken the name "XpressionsoftheHeart.com."

Step-father, mother, step-mother, father

A GIFT

From: _____

To: _____

Presented: _____

Date: _____

WHY I WROTE THE BOOK

Take the first step and read this introduction page. Consider the information, ideas and approaches presented in this book as seeds in a garden – and you are the gardener. My desire is that **YOU** cultivate these seeds and apply them to your unique situations, making your academic and professional careers more productive. I will not be able to convince and inspire all of you; some of you don't need convincing. But if I can convince a few, then my book is **PAID-IN-FULL**.

STRAIGHT TALK – "STIMULATING IDEAS FOR TRUE ACADEMIC DEVELOPMENT" was envisioned in 1984 while I was attending Grambling State University in Grambling, Louisiana. Serving as sophomore class president, I became affiliated with the National Alliance of Business Industry Cluster Program and the National Urban League's Black Executive Exchange Program. In both organizations, I served as student president. But more importantly, I was introduced to innovative approaches that strengthened the link between business, industry, government and education. Both student-oriented programs were vehicles in which Grambling State University superimposed an academic setting into a business environment. It was then that I became keenly aware that individuals have a personal responsibility to be willing participants in preparing for career opportunities.

Some will ask, "Why have you written this book?" My question is different: "How could I not have written this book?" There is a time to stand up and be counted – to stand up and offer one's best to make a difference. I've written this book not because I've achieved a certain level of financial status. It is because I finally got MAD! I Made A Decision to Make A Difference. It is because the message is timely and others need to know RIGHT NOW to get footing on the path to success!

Through trial and error, I've painstakingly developed some valuable skills over the years making countless mistakes along the way. Hence this book was written to address these specific issues and concerns.

◆ Alert students to critical issues that are not taught in the course of a formal education and only learned through experience, hard knocks and observation.
◆ Inspire excellence in students, career transitioners, corporate climbers or anyone who desires to achieve a greater level of success and happiness.
◆ Provide spiritual food for nourishment, growth and maturity to compliment the contents in each chapter.

I urge you to use this book in the spirit of "preparation meets opportunity." It is the reader's responsibility to prepare and cultivate a fertile ground for his or her mental garden. Digest these seeds into your daily activities and take the initiative to share these seeds with your friends, family or colleagues. As your seeds continue to grow, you will create real, lasting value in your life and make long-lasting influences on others as well. Never underestimate the impression you may make on others.

Whose life have you touched today? Why not pass this on? I just did.

Turn the page and explore the journey with me. The journey is yours to live, experience and fulfill. Enjoy the rest of the trip as you read the book from cover to cover!

Harlynn LaVance Hammonds
Email: LaVance@xpressionsoftheheart.com
Web: http://www.xpressionsoftheheart.com

"Stimulate Your Mind With Knowledge"

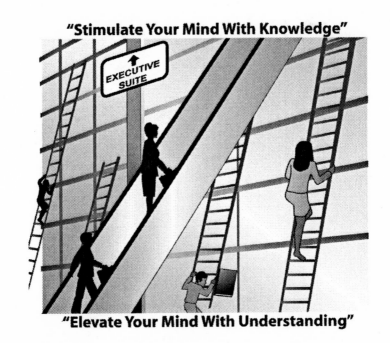

"Elevate Your Mind With Understanding"

PROVERBS 15:22 - "Plans fail for lack of counsel, but with many advisors they succeed."

MATTHEW 7: 13-14 - "Enter through the narrow gate. For wide is the gate and broad is the road that leads to destruction, and many enter through it. But small is the gate and narrow the road that leads to life, and only a few find it."

CHAPTER 1: THE SIGNIFICANCE OF A GOOD EDUCATION

Nothing gives YOU more of an advantage than the attainment of an education. Regardless of what it is that motivates individuals to seek a higher education, a good education is the key that opens the doors of opportunity. So complete your bachelor's, pursue your master's, earn a professional diploma, or simply update your skills and expertise to maintain your marketability.

The Road To Success Is Paved With A Good Education

The reasons for wanting a college education are as diverse as the people who seek to gain a degree. Some very important reasons for going to college are:

- To learn a specific educational discipline or new technology.
- To boost earning power.
- To increase job security.
- Career advancement.
- Self-fulfillment.

Don't let excuses and obstacles keep you from earning that degree or learning a new skill. If you have the will to get an education, you will find a way to obtain it through face-to-face instructions in a classroom environment, on-the-job training or an online "virtual classroom." **If not now…when?**

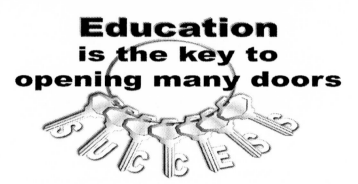

WHY IS EDUCATION IMPORTANT?

Earning your degree has never been so critical. In today's extraordinarily competitive business environment, more people are vying for fewer positions. Employers look at your training and academic credentials more closely than ever. Without question, an education is paramount for future success and acquired knowledge opens the door to good jobs and a better future.

One of the basic bargaining tools we have is the amount of knowledge we possess. The pursuit of educational goals and priorities will help you navigate through the vast opportunities, unlimited possibilities, and awesome challenges that await you. We are living in the greatest period of change the world has ever known. Acquiring new knowledge to replace existing knowledge is vital to keeping pace with the information explosion that's now taking place. Change is continuous, and our ability to adapt and grasp new functions is more critical today than it was yesterday.

The message is clear! Education bridges the emerging gap between the relatively low skills of new workers compared to the advancing skill requirements of the new economy. An investment in knowledge gives you the best dividends simply because "to earn more, you have to learn more." **However, a vast majority of students have a yearning for earning but not a yearning for learning.**

In the rush of technological changes, we often overlook the point that education is much more than gained knowledge, its APPLIED KNOWLEDGE. Essentially, an education and acquired knowledge do the following:

- Create both new wants and the necessary skills to make a living in tomorrow's technologically advanced world.
- Propel an individual upward in career, social and economic status.
- Provide a hedge against failure and act as a prescription for survival.
- Allow adaptability to change.

Also, it is very important to know that the biggest and most profound changes coming are societal, economical, political and religious. New legal, ethical, commercial and philosophical issues will strain our institutions to the limit. Moral questions are beginning to tear at the foundation of our value systems.

All of these are reasons why we need to establish educational priorities and strive for academic excellence in our lives. This book was written to provide tips on how to succeed in this brutal economic world.

HERE IS A "FUNNY" STORY that illustrates the importance of education. It was listed in *Bits & Pieces*, Volume 56, a magazine that motivates the world. The author is unknown.

"What are we going to do?" said Baby Tiger to Mama Tiger in the jungle. "Here comes a hunter, and he has five rifles, three special sighting scopes, and devices to allow him to see in the dark!"

"Hush!" answered Mama Tiger, and she taught her cub how to sneak up from behind and pounce. The hunter was never heard of again. All of which goes to prove that technology may be fine, but it will never be a substitute for a good, basic education.

DID YOU KNOW – What you should really get out of your educational experience is the discipline and the process of acquiring new knowledge? Others can assist you in the learning process, but you must do the learning. Think of your education as a process of learning how to learn, learning how to keep an open mind and learning about the relationship between yourself and your environment. Rather than absorb masses of information that will become outdated tomorrow, young people in schools today must learn information and communication skills that will serve them as lifelong learners.

To become a learner, you must learn how to find, evaluate, analyze and synthesize information. Learning how to learn, think, and act are the key objectives on which you must focus your attention. This attribute alone is essential to gaining a quality education.

The business world wants educated, competitive and well-trained graduates – individuals who can acquire new knowledge and adapt to new roles. They want people with a full range of professional and personal skills – not just pure theoretical understanding. Specific skills include exercising good judgment, making wise decisions, getting along with and leading others. The specifics of what you are learning may, in a sense, be less important than your understanding of how to learn.

In tomorrow's job market, training and learning will not stop when a full-time career begins. A rapidly changing economy means a need for lifelong learning. These four points will keep you focused on your educational and training objectives:

- In today's competitive environment, you have to keep learning and growing in knowledge.
- Your field of endeavor is not critical to how successful you can become. It is the way in which you approach your endeavor that matters. Find mentors - in your company, in your industry - who want to see you do well.
- Proactively manage your skill development and, ultimately, your career. Make your personal learning and career development a priority.
- To get ahead, you must have the right credentials and networking contacts. Many jobs come from "know-who" rather than "know-how."

The continuing pursuit of knowledge and current standards/practices within a professional discipline is a must. Continue to read publications to stay up-to-date on different professions and join professional organizations to keep you in touch with the latest developments in your field. Never stop learning and never stop growing and expanding as a person in your endeavors. Arming yourself with pertinent information assures you will be prepared to seize success when the opportunity knocks. Being better trained and better educated positions you to earn more income.

Students – The Missing Dimension In Education

The aim and objective of our educational system is to develop the **TOTAL STUDENT**. To do this, we must have the complete cooperation of the student in being an active participant in their educational experience. The missing dimension in education is the lack of personal responsibility, non-participation and an inner desire to achieve by students while attending school.

The needs of our colleges and universities are great and their resources limited; therefore, students need to be more active and responsible for their own objectives and actions. The approach behind this student-oriented improvement program is to bring fresh, new ideas and perspectives to the decision table. In this process, students develop goal direction and goal awareness that makes them more receptive to the aims and objectives of the university. When that happens, there is a significant increase in student activities and participation. As Dr. Mabel Phiefer, professor at Howard University said, "The greater the level of involvement, the greater the support; the greater the support, the greater the vested interest." This helps in discovering perhaps the most important quality of college life itself – students having individualism, identification, vision, motivation, desire to learn and ambition to succeed.

College is more than sporting paraphernalia that boasts school colors and fraternal memberships. Emphasis should be placed on a vibrant and healthy collegiate environment that combines strong academic achievement with relevant social activities. One may argue that demanding course schedules promote lack of participation in school activities; however, this argument carries little weight, especially when students adjust academic schedules to participate in activities of special interest such as dancing, sports, pledging, band practice, etc. If you neglect activities and fail to express interest and participate in school activities, participation in activities of corporate business culture will be foreign to you.

To get more specific, our interest in activities like organizational meetings, conferences and workshops, seminars, and school elections should have top priority. Participation in these activities should be a personal requirement for every student in making their voices heard. The habit of getting involved should be digested into your daily schedule of activities.

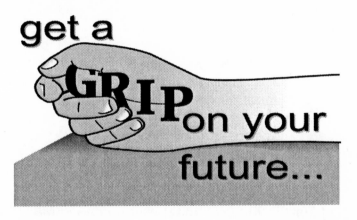

Student recommendations are necessary for implementation of a positive plan toward improving the overall efficiency and effectiveness of universities. The responsibilities of college students are numerous and sometimes overwhelming. This generation of students has the personal responsibilities of:

- Pursuing educational objectives and sound academic principles as aggressively and purposely as possible.
- Accepting the intellectual challenge and demonstrating a passion for learning. This responsibility belongs to students who want to learn.
- Carrying the torch of personal excellence to achieve dreams, hopes and ambitions.
- Sharing lessons from observations or participation with other students to make their transition easier and more successful.

- Demonstrating commitment in supporting activities that enrich college life.
- Developing and implementing continuing solutions to issues confronted in our academic institutions.

I encourage you to examine your educational priorities and opportunities a little closer, as I had to do while attending Grambling State University. I realized my academic endeavors were not in sync with my educational priorities. Unfortunately and unnecessarily, my examination occurred too late and resulted in academic probation, then suspension and loss of a scholarship. That was my turning point, my awakening. The reality of what happened hit me like a bolt of lightning. This reality assessment presented an opportunity to show real character and move forward by hitting the books with a new resolve. After returning to school and enrollment in Air Force ROTC, I reconditioned my attitude, realigned my priorities, initiated self disciple and mental strength, earned national dean's recognition and graduated with honors in May, 1985 as a commissioned officer.

This experience urges me to say, "The majority of students tend to be observers of their education rather than participants." Too often, students just want to put in their time. This narrow view may reflect an attitude that can hurt your academic progression. People who have a college education often take it for granted, and they are disappointed when it does not prove to be a substitute for working hard. All an education does is open a mind; it does not fill an empty one.

The issue of pursuing and obtaining an education is serious business. The responsibilities lie with you to make your college years a meaningful and learning experience. How you approach the rest of your college experience will set a pattern for your lifetime. Make sure this pattern includes the appreciation of learning as a continuing and unending process. Fortunately, our education does not end just because we leave school. Life itself is a classroom – everything that happens to us, both **POSITIVE** and **NEGATIVE**.

> **APPLIED KNOWLEDGE IS REAL POWER!**
> If You Think Education Is Expensive – Try Education Without Execution. Knowledge Demands Responsibility and Responsibility Demands Accountability!

Please refer to Appendix 1 (page 95) for corresponding spiritual scriptures.

CHAPTER 2: ACHIEVING GOALS AND PLANNING FOR SUCCESS

As a college student or corporate employee, you face the challenge of being well prepared for that job. The dizzy pace at which the world is changing makes nearly all choices of occupation somewhat risky, which underlines the importance of setting goals and carefully choosing your academic discipline. The importance of focusing on achieving goals and planning for success is essential to college achievement, graduation and, ultimately, career advancement.

All successful individuals have established goals. No one, including myself, will get anywhere without a consuming purpose, plan and goal. So if you don't have it, get it and get it quickly! Aim for the highest goals and use your finest instincts to reach those goals. When you discover what it is that you really want and you are persistently focused on obtaining it, the unleashing of incredible imagination and power will help you visualize yourself in possession of these things.

Purpose, goals and success are entities. They are dependent on each other for an individual to continuously accomplish his or her task. Robert Allen, author of "Power of Purpose," indicates, "When you are on purpose, nothing will stop you. Purpose is more important than money, and goals without purpose have no power. When you are not, any distraction, problem obstacle, disappointment, negative thought or feeling can divert you." To achieve goals and become successful, learn to focus passionately and unfalteringly on the process of achieving your goals. This will energize you with motivation, inspiration, passion and a commitment to keep growing, learning and discovering.

Ignite Your Purpose with Goal Setting

Let me first say … without clearly defined goals, you will not achieve the success you want. Success in any area of your life – be it personal or business – starts with a goal. Without setting goals, you stagnate too quickly! Let me ask you two questions.

◆ How **SMART** are you?
◆ Are your goals **S**pecific, **M**easurable, **A**ttainable, **R**ealistic, and **T**angible?

Simply, goals are captured by those who develop enthusiastic determination to follow through with their plan, regardless of what other people say, think or do. Consistent action develops the momentum principle of success. As you move forward in accomplishing your goals, the more self-motivated and resourceful you will become.

Clearly defined, written goals will turn the power of your mind into a laser beam, drawing you closer to opportunities, people, and knowledge that will help you navigate the obstacles along your success path.

Set goals that are high enough to excite you, yet near enough to keep in sight. If you possess any conflicting beliefs to your goals, you will not succeed. Questions to ask that will challenge your thinking and beliefs are:

- ◆ What goals do you want to achieve?
- ◆ What is the significant purpose of achieving your goals?
- ◆ Can you see yourself successfully completing the goals you are striving for?
- ◆ How important is planning to your daily activities?
- ◆ Why are you not at your goal already?
- ◆ Do you have goals that inspire you?
- ◆ What amount of effort are you willing to commit to turn your goals into reality?
- ◆ How important is it to prepare for your college career?
- ◆ Are you worthy of your goals?

The goals you set are a prelude to action and a track to run on. Goals are the expressions of one's desire to achieve, to improve circumstances and to be even better tomorrow than you are today. Before you are able to create a plan, you must first define your objectives in terms of what you plan to accomplish. Formulate goals that are realistic and attainable. Make a list of your goals – not someone else's - both short and long term. Decide exactly what you want to achieve in a given time to measure your progress, and tell yourself that you can and will pursue your goals with excitement. This tends to impress goals on your memory and convinces your goal-setting, subconscious mind that you mean business. After you have written down your goals, go a step further and actually "see" them as accomplished facts. Take a few minutes and visualize yourself in possession of those things. Creative visualization or mental imaging helps to reinforce your goals.

When you consciously focus on achieving goals, it gives you at least three distinct advantages over a person who wanders aimlessly. **FIRST**, a goal specifically focuses you, even in your sleep, to find ways to achieve it. **SECOND**, it gives you additional enthusiasm and provides you with the catalyst you need to maintain motivation. And **THIRD**, it gives you direction when you are confused or lost.

Where Are You In Relationship To Your Goals?

As you look at what you have accomplished thus far, it may occur to you that the outcome is different from the goals you had established for yourself. Goals are merely conceptual. Outcome is reality. Outcome is the direct result you created because you approached goal setting in a systematic and disciplinary way. In determining the effectiveness of your actions or efforts, simply evaluate your outcome.

Many lessons will be learned. Unfortunately, too many people squander their resources looking for the quick fix – the short cut – to achieving their goals.

Many people routinely do things – or they fail to do things without even knowing it. Face the reality; in spite of what you think, you may well be using the entirely wrong approach ... and not even know it!!! Most people fail to accomplish their goals simply because they repeat their old mistakes and repeat them harder and faster. What one must do when these things happen – and they usually will – is simply get back on track by adjusting your approach to keep moving forward in a positive direction. Look at this as a personal performance audit like a balance sheet which quickly informs you of your assets and liabilities.

Formulate goals that are realistic and attainable. A very important factor in your future achievement is **WHERE YOU ARE NOW** in relationship to your goals. These **five basic steps** will help to focus your specific goals:

- Identify your goal and prioritize goals worth your time.
- Determine where you are in embracing your goals.
- Keep in mind where you want to be – your destination point. Are my tasks consistent with my primary goal? Will my task actually help me achieve my primary goal?
- Set a specific time limit for obtaining your goal.
- Practice short jumps, keeping your eye on your purpose and goals.

For the moment, I want you to forget about what you may lack. What ultimately matters is what you make happen. The **"THOMAS Principle"** described below can be valuable in determining where you are in relationship to your support system. In considering the THOMAS Principle, never limit yourself or limit your thoughts. When there are no limitations, there are no limiting goals. Simply, the **"THOMAS Principle"** is:

- Lack of **T**ime
- Lack of **H**ealth
- Lack of **O**pportunity
- Lack of **M**oney
- Lack of **A**bility
- Lack of **S**upport – from family, friends, colleagues or loved ones.

14

In most situations, time and money will be the roadblocks to reaching your goals. Continue pressing on, realizing that obstacles are seldom the same size tomorrow as they are today.

Planning for Success

Success means many different things to most of us. What does success mean to you? To this writer, success is living your life with personal and financial freedom combined with a humble attitude of gratitude to:

- Servicing the community.
- Adding value to the society.
- Empowering others to grow and prosper.

It is certainly not the ultimate destination, but a journey filled with determined focus, sacrifices, careful planning and a relentless positive attitude to fulfill your dreams. Achieving success means expecting success and doing daily what unsuccessful people do occasionally. In other words, success is a continuous marathon to pursue personal triumphs and overcome the challenges of life with enthusiasm and persistence. Slow and steady, not a sprint, wins the race.

Many, many great writers have written thousands of articles on this subject, but none have described the success formula better than W. Clement Stone who said, "There is very little difference between success and failure – the little difference is your attitude, the big difference is whether your attitude is positive or negative. It is your choice." Your attitude impacts everything you do and it is your internal compass to designing an extraordinary life or mediocre life.

There are different ways of planning for success. One way is to say, "Here is my goal" and then to continue down a road irrespective of what is happening in your surrounding environment. The other way is to make a plan and expect it to change.

Review your plans on a regular basis. This is necessary because changes will infringe on your plans. New action plans and deadlines may be required to sail past obstacles or breeze through opportunities. Your plans will serve as a road map to lead you from the starting point to your final destination and, ultimately, achievement of your goals. Therefore, you must continuously re-evaluate your plans because life's experiences do not evolve around fixed, static circumstances or situations.

It is very important to know what you want! A study of high achievers reveals that they:

- Know exactly what they want to accomplish.
- Possess an unshakeable conviction that they can do it.
- Work doggedly and persistently until they achieve their goals.

Just remember ... Prior Proper Planning Prevents Piss Poor Performance. Lack of planning leads to crisis management, and crisis management leads to insufficient time for planning.

Getting Back On Track

The hardest part of resetting your sights on your goals is getting out of a rut and letting go of your fear of failure. Most of the time, we sit and wait for someone else to lead or to give us the power to turn our vision into reality. Don't let **F.E.A.R (False Evidence Appearing Real)** keep you from attaining your hopes, dreams and goals. Fears of failure are stumbling blocks that you can overcome. Without failure, there is no learning and no growth. It is by finding out what does not work that we learn what does.

If you go astray, don't be too harsh or critical of yourself, but realize your failures and let your mistakes rest in peace. Stay resilient through the challenges of life to overcome chronic negativity.

◆ Be fearless in your journey to greatness.
◆ Be fearless in knowing what you want.
◆ Be fearless in your visions and passions.
◆ Be fearless in taking risks but be prepared to deal with the outcome.

You Can Find Unlimited Excuses For Failure, But No One Ever Makes An Excuse For Success. To be successful we must wipe the dust off our dreams and bring them back into our sights. I am living proof of this and sincerely believe you can recapture your long-lost goals. Vividly I remember when my career derailed. I could no longer visualize my goals, dreams and ambitions. They simply got lost in my daily struggles to survive. For years I struggled, plunging deeper and deeper into depression because my actions kept building up negative momentum. Failure (unexpected results) was tattooed on my forehead, and I didn't have a clue how to get back on track with job stability and economic parity. My passion and heart's desire were lying dormant within me, and I had no fire to fuel my lack of motivation, enthusiasm and money.

In comparison, this is similar to a valuable item sitting on a shelf collecting dust – that was my dilemma. I became detached from my passion to lead, motivate, inspire and enable others to achieve their goals. It was during this time in my life that I recognized and learned a valuable lesson: people succeed or fail one decision at a time! The choices you make will undoubtedly impact your path in life for better or worse - propelling you into a life of abundance and prosperity or can devastate your wellness and financial foundation. The end result of your choices becomes self evident over time – some are more immediate that others.

If you understand and apply only one fundamental principle from this book, get this one principle. Find your area of excellence and what it is that brings you inner joy and fulfillment. This will ignite an inner fire to reconnect with your vision and passion – your sense of purpose to fuel your uncompromising commitment to excellence. Connecting daily with your passion directs you to your calling and inspires you to do more, be a better individual and become who you were meant to be. Reinforce your area of excellence with creative visualization and confirm it with constant repetition of positive affirmations (mental-rehearsal) until it's accepted in your mind. Then enthusiastically act on it to achieve your goal or desired outcome. Motivational speaker Dennis Kimbro says that we should take the statement, "I'll believe it when I see it," at face value. Always remember that poor is a state of mind – an attitude – but broke is only a temporary condition.

Getting back on track depends on your level of self-discipline to overcome resistance, obstacles, setbacks, challenges and bridges with low clearances. No plan can possibly work if you fail to pursue your goals with strength, perseverance, integrity and unwavering faith. When self-discipline is combined with "new" positive attitudes, getting and staying motivated are key drivers to putting your dreams, hopes and aspirations back into action. The ability to stay focused on your chosen work will prevent roadblocks and disappointments from inhibiting your life's destiny and purpose.

Very few people have been able to avoid failure, setbacks or mistakes in their pursuit of obtaining success. Mistakes are failed attempts to get it right. Failure breeds success. If you encounter failure or mistakes, the surest way to harness success is to engage your fall-back plan, then move ahead through small wins and small failures. Quickly learn and recuperate when you experience failure, resistance, obstacles, setbacks or mistakes. Each time you spring back into action, you are better equipped to deal with these challenging issues. Each small win triggers an attitude that embraces "I can do it," "I can make it happen." View your challenges as opportunities to grow, learn and develop new choices to adapt and pursue alternative paths.

As you attain one dream, it sows the seeds for the next one. As Michael Kelly, a nationally acclaimed personal development coach, so eloquently said, "Opportunity is wherever I am, and every day I expect new things to happen that will open the way to my success."

When it comes to achieving dreams, people either adjust their dreams to fit their means, or they adjust their means to fit their dreams. The successful ones are motivated to adjust their means to achieve their dreams. Most people have no problem dreaming; however, an empowered dream is one that you need and are willing to work hard to attain. But most of us avoid having empowered dreams because we don't want to desire something so badly that we can't live without it – because then if we can't get it, what are we going to do?

Success Is Within Your Reach

Success in any area of life is achieved by identifying optimum strategies and repeating them until they become habits. Success doesn't happen overnight – only in rare situations like winning the lottery or capitalizing on the stock market is there immediate financial gain with no effort!

Many dream of great successes. Some succeed because they are destined to, but most succeed because they are determined to succeed. The most successful individuals are not necessarily those who work the hardest or longest hours or who have the better grades or better advice. Successful individuals have the knowledge to succeed, implement a plan to succeed and consistently follow the plan to achieve measurable results and accomplishments. Successful individuals are those who master the classroom of life with persistence and endurance in the face of difficult odds despite the puzzling and elusive, inherit nature of achieving success. Successful individuals are those who have the capacity to grow and learn how to manage their personal and professional lives.

Let Michael Kelly's words – "Success is not just getting there, it is earning the right to be there" – echo in your mind. Your plan for success depends on your level of self-discipline to stay committed and motivated in following an ongoing system for success. This system consists of patience, time and guidance from others who have treaded similar waters. Whether pursuing professional success or high performance in personal goals, expect to succeed. Expectation energizes your goals and gives them momentum. Persist until you succeed.

Persistence will ensure that you achieve your goal, but persistence in the wrong thoughts or practices will sabotage your efforts to reach your goals. It is critical that you have the right road map and the proper vehicle before starting your journey. No matter how hard one persists, faulty maps are often at the root of most failures. Practice small steps to produce immediate and noticeable results. This allows you to minimize your risks and lets you verify your assumptions and projections, no matter how uncertain your venture.

Successful people have these qualities in common:

- ◆ They are **self motivated,** putting forth a sustained and persistent effort toward accomplishing their goals.
- ◆ They radiate a **positive "can-do" attitude**.
- ◆ They are **goal-directed, organized** and **execute around priorities**.
- ◆ They are **observant, detailed-oriented** and **do ordinary things exceptionally well.**
- ◆ They **effectively manage and leverage their time to accomplish more in less time**.
- ◆ They **maximize their earning power and build leverage into money-making activities**.
- ◆ They implement a **system others have used to create wealth and health.**

W. Clement Stone, philanthropist and author of *The Success System That Never Fails*, says there are 10 major steps necessary to convert your past failures to successes and achieve future goals:

- ◆ Write down the goals you definitely want to achieve.
- ◆ Take a half hour each day to review your written goals, and list ideas that flash into your mind.
- ◆ Keep your mind on what you want and off what you do not want.
- ◆ Picture yourself already in possession of your goal – creative visualization.
- ◆ Try to recognize, relate, assimilate and apply principles from what you see, hear, read, think or experience in your environment.

- Look for the principles that are applicable to you to develop better physical, mental and moral health, wealth and the true riches of life.
- Use suggestions to influence others and self-suggestion with regularity.
- Memorize quotations that will inspire you.
- Learn how to help yourself, and share your knowledge and blessings with others.
- When you have a worthy thought that flashes to mind, write it down, then implement it.

Truth be told, success comes from an accumulation of a lot of little things that quickly mushroom together to build fuel for action. Achieving success is not so much a matter of how much savvy, intelligence, education or inborn attributes one has. Achieving success is not even a matter of how much financial wizardry, technical superiority, or organizational ability you have. And, it is not dependent on the application of some magic formula or deceptive, unethical financial practices. Rather, it depends on how you persistently and systematically approach your opportunities, obstacles and possibilities. Success is determined by ones' ability to adapt and act in an effective manner – to execute around priorities to accomplish the desired outcome.

If success has always been elusive to you, maybe it's time to change your approach.

> **Get serious about your life and achievement of worthwhile goals. Have a vision of your future and create goals consistent with that vision.**
> **Life will not go according to plan if you have no plan. The realization of your dreams is a choice – the power of choice is yours!**

Please refer to Appendix 2 (page 99) for corresponding spiritual scriptures.

CHAPTER 3: THE SKY'S THE LIMIT
PERSONALITY

These words may sound familiar and to some it may sound a little intimidating. It's often said, "The greatest tragedy is to become less than your full potential – using less than the abilities you have to work with." Regardless of present external circumstances, you can develop the innate qualities necessary to be among those who are successful and winners of their challenges. Winners expect to win; losers dream about what winners feel like when they win.

An underlying factor that separates those who succeed and fail is simply your attitude – your frame of mind and self-confidence. Your attitude (negative or positive) influences everything you do and everything you say. Nurture your positive thoughts and they will have a profound effect on your life purpose, causing you to build your motivation to overflowing levels.

Dare To Dream Big – Personal Empowerment

Dream a little … just for a moment would you?

Years ago, I had a dream, but it was only a list of goals. There was something missing. I was living my life at the mercy of others, hoping my day was going to come. I then learned life has so much to offer, if you dare to seek it. When an individual finds the courage to take action and make a difference, one then recognizes that living in a comfort zone yields too little challenge.

Everyone has something that motivates and inspires their will to act. Despite all opposition and obstacles, don't abandon your dreams, hopes and ambitions. You can make them come true. You can revive your long-lost dreams, hopes and ambitions as you rediscover the positive, motivated and successful person hidden within you. **IT'S UP TO YOU!** It really is true – your future does lie in your hands. **If you Challenge Your Mind Power, it will Ignite The Heart To Dream. If you Dare To Dream It, Dare To Achieve It!** The **realization of your dreams and fulfillment of life purpose IS POSSIBLE**...if you **Dare to Dream Big ... Set Your Loftiest Goals – And Put Your Dreams Into Action To Achieve Every Goal You Aspire With Excellence and Greatness**.

Often we struggle to find balance, passion and fulfillment in our personal and professional lives. As I experienced in my struggles, you may feel stuck in your daily activities, your job, family obligations and financial obligations. You are not alone. Each day, virtually millions of people go to work only because they have to. They go through the motions of performing tasks they literally hate. Not only are they miserable, but they are also less than productive. Why do they repeat the routine day in and day out? They allowed circumstances to stick them into a slot where they'll remain until they experience a change in attitude or until they cease to exist. They've allowed others to set goals for them. They've fallen into the trap of conformity that destroys initiative and independence and suppresses the inner drive for self-fulfillment and satisfaction.

Instead, people should not be pushed or pulled toward a certain fate but should be motivated from within. Many things in our life are easy to discard. Dreams and aspirations are not. Pursue the things that catch your heart not your eye, whatever that may be regardless of age or experience. Follow your passion then pursue it with all the time and talent the Creator has given you. In your heart you know there is something special to accomplish. What a person does is the outcome of what that individual thinks or feels.

- Are you capable of doing more than what you are accomplishing?
- Do you wake up enthused each morning about your school, work and daily activities?
- Do you believe you are a winner and have a rock solid will to succeed beyond your dreams?
- Is your walk in life filled with purpose, power and passion?
- Are your actions attracting positive expressions from others?

Walter D. Scott of Northwestern University said, "Success or failure in any undertaking is caused more by mental attitude than mental capacity." Your attitude controls your future. It changes as you perceive what you want to be and what you ought not to be.

Picture the world in front of you, ready to become the reality of your dreams, ready to stage your desires. You must believe in the power of your thoughts because the eyes only see what the mind comprehends and achieves. Visualize your vision or passion them empower it with your belief system and enthusiasm to actualize and accomplish your objectives. Success comes to those who think about success and strive for it. A person will never be anything unless he or she knows what he or she wants to be. This is a fact in personal life, and the same is true in business or in your career. You will hardly achieve unless you know what you want to achieve. You can make real and lasting attitude changes by making a conscious, determined choice combined with diligent, planned actions focused on what you want to achieve.

When you are conditioning yourself for success, focus on qualities you already possess and develop them into assets that will help you achieve happiness and success. Let me remind you of valuable words spoken by Denis Waitley, a peak performer consultant, who says, "Genuine lasting success comes from nurturing your own special talents, recognizing your natural abilities, and learning to live fully with your own inward thoughts, attitudes and ideals."

One key point is that few people recognize an opportunity because it is usually disguised as hard work. Many times we let opportunities slip past us because we are still considering them. The primary objective is to create them as you see them. If you do not see them, it is because you have closed your eyes to them. It is a matter of identifying your goals and not being distracted from achieving them. Dennis Kimbro, author of *Think and Grow Rich – A Black Choice*, offers words that are appropriate. Kimbro says, "Opportunity first takes shape in your mind. You must be ready to take advantage of all opportunities, not only when opportunity knocks at your door, but be ready to knock on opportunity's door." Windows of opportunity open and close quickly!

Remember, your dreams are the things you desire, not a burden someone else has given you. You will find that your **dreams can be classified into five categories**:

- What would you like to have or own?
- Where would you like to go or travel?
- What would you like to do or create?
- What would you like to be or become?
- What would you like to contribute or give back?

Whatever your dreams and desires, they require a concerted effort to create the momentum to make them happen. Each item on your dream list is merely a latent reality that simply requires nurturing and time to materialize. The question is not whether your dreams will happen but whether you are ready, willing and able to give birth to their attainment.

- Are you ready to commit yourself to the self-discipline that requires goal-setting, planning and maintaining a positive mental attitude to make your dreams come true?

27

◆ Are you ready to secure your dreams with persistence?

Every morning you should wake with exhilaration and excitement to face the day and prepare for the tasks at hand.

Develop "Can Do" Winning Attitudes

As you consider the success you desire and embrace the reality of your perception, you will affirm its possibilities and develop the self-confidence of top achievers. The power of thought is limitless when you give your thoughts effective expression. This compels your vision or mission to activate positive mind thoughts that provide creative visualization for what you want to accomplish, do or become. You will be astounded at your results as you begin to see the picture completed. And finally, you must be able to radiate and infect others with your positive attitude. Communicate your ideas so others can share your vision and see the power of your thoughts. Communicate with others to make them feel special in your presence.

CAN-DO
WINNING
ATTITUDES
(From the "The Executive Gallery – Positive Can-Do Attitude Series")

CAN'T	**CAN DO**
We've never done it before.	We have the opportunity to be first.
It's too complicated.	Let's look at it from a different angle.
We don't have the resources.	Necessity is the mother of invention.
It will never work.	We'll give it a try.
There isn't enough time.	We'll reevaluate some priorities.
We've already tried it.	We learned from the experience.

There's no way it will work.	We can make it work.
It's a waste of time.	Think of the possibilities.
It's a waste of money.	The investment will be worth it.
We'll cannibalize our own sales.	We'll do it before they do.
We don't have the experience.	Let's network with those who do.
We can't compete.	We'll get a jump on the competition.
Our vendor won't go for it.	Let's show them the opportunities.
We're understaffed.	We're a lean, mean machine.
We don't have enough room.	Temporary space may be an option.
It will never fly.	We'll never know until we try.
No one communicates.	Let's open the channels.
It can't be done.	It will be a challenge.
Our company is the wrong size.	We're perfect for this project.
It takes too long for approvals.	We'll walk it through the system.
It's too radical a change.	Let's take a chance.
We don't have the equipment.	Maybe we can sub it out.
Isn't it time to go home?	Days go so quickly around here.
It's contrary to policy.	Anything is possible.
It's not my job.	I'll be glad to take the responsibility.
I don't have any idea.	I'll come up with some alternatives.
Our customers won't buy it.	We'll do a better job at educating them.
Let somebody else deal with it.	I'm ready to learn something new.
We don't have enough money.	Maybe there's something we can cut?
It's not going to get any better.	We'll try it one more time.
We're always changing directions.	We're in touch with our customers.

I CAN'T   I CAN

Aggressive, motivated individuals should make a note of this motivational message. The following excerpt was taken from *The Challenge*, written by Dr. Marilyn Wilkes Granger: "I have the ability to succeed. Therefore, I will do it! I have the ability to achieve excellence. Therefore, I will achieve it! I have the ability to think positively. Therefore, I will do it! If I have to I

29

can do anything! My strength is derived from my determination.
I am indestructible. I am whoever and whatever I wish to be! I
will learn and I will succeed!"

Remember … motivation without inspiration never last.

Get and stay motivated to achieve any goal.
Believe in yourself and see the possibilities in
your life. Manage your life and your
environment. You can, and should, set your
goals and unleash your passion to keep
achieving your goals, one after another.

**Please refer to Appendix 3 (page 102) for corresponding
spiritual scriptures.**

CHAPTER 4: PERSONAL AND CAREER DEVELOPMENT

Careers just don't happen – they are planned. Planning for a successful career should start as soon as you enter college. Each year should be a stage for developing your career path. The objective is to pursue your education as aggressively and purposefully as possible. College introduces you to information that will enhance your intellectual capabilities, and it will act as a stimulus to motivate and develop you to the fullest.

Stuck At The Crossroads

HOW YOU HANDLE THE REALITIES OF TODAY WILL AFFECT THE POSSIBILITIES OF TOMORROW

One of the most important commitments you will ever make is the commitment to your personal and career development. This experience can prove to be a valuable stepping stone in making your college years challenging, stimulating and productive.

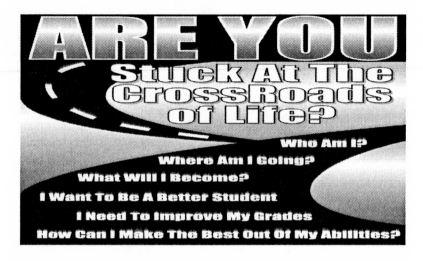

If you think you are confused, consider poor Columbus. He did not know where he was going, and when he got there, he did not know where he was. When he got back, he did not know where he had been. College years are very similar to the journey of Columbus. Your life can't go according to plan if you have no plan.

College Freshmen – One Step At A Time

> **Quote** – author unknown: "The higher the goal, the harder the climb. But taken each day, one step at a time, the goal is accomplished, the dream is attained and the wisdom and strength are gained."

The earlier years of undergraduate studies can be one of the scariest and most exciting times of your life. Not only is it competitive, but it is also a time of career exploration. It is a time to assess your priorities and values and match your winning attitude with your winning behavior.

The initial step of your academic journey is to start accepting responsibility for who you are, what you have today and everything that happens to you. Immediate responsibility is the best training ground for future responsibility. In the crucial, formative years of college, your career development should be focused on sharpening your interpersonal and academic skills, establishing self-confidence and learning all you can. Your belief that you will succeed at the beginning of your freshman term will be the one thing that assures the successful outcome of your collegiate journey.

Observe the tips below to focus on your academic endeavors:

- Start your college life with a purpose to succeed and keep moving that purpose to higher marks as you academically progress through your college years.
- Keep your educational aim in sight. In your daily activities, strive for excellence in the classroom. You shouldn't spend time complaining, but spend time studying and embracing your academic goals. Too many of your peers will become experts in football and fraternities rather than in business, math, science, history and the arts.
- Tap into your academic advisor and instructors' real-world business expertise to learn all you can about careers and career opportunities.
- Get the most out of your educational dollars. Planning and preparing for your educational success is not an overnight or a one-time effort. You must believe the hours spent studying and the efforts put into it will make a difference between academic success and failure.
- Fine-tune your learning techniques and study skills to develop critical and analytical thinking. There are tools, techniques and methods to help you learn how to study, take and organize notes. Writing papers, note taking, reading, making oral presentations, power reading, test taking, managing time, problem solving and improving memory are skills associated with achievement in learning. Establish a study schedule that works for you

– don't be influenced by the study habits of your peers. Small improvements in study skills pay big dividends.

◆ Take the toughest courses to challenge your mind power. Break your assignments into manageable pieces to deal with work overload. Consequently, you can envision more tangible results from a vigorous academic challenge.

◆ Improve your concentration and stop "mind wandering" on outside distractions that interfere with effective learning. Listen and concentrate so that you can understand what is being said. The key is self-discipline. Without it, your accomplishments will be few; with it, anything is within your grasp.

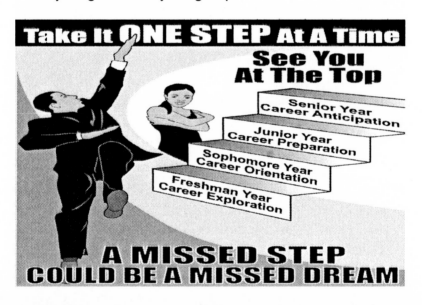

To make the best of your college years, you have to take a personal inventory of your academic goals. I challenge you to aggressively study and seek thrills, not in drugs or sex, but in achieving position and control over your own destiny. Your future is purchased today. Prepare today for an exciting, successful tomorrow. The environment you are now in is only but a small fraction of the real test you will face in the business world.

Moreover, you cannot afford to settle for mere survival. Survival is necessary but not sufficient. You need success and success in today's world demands excellence. You can do it! You can excel and maximize your potential. You can be #1 in other areas besides entertainment and sports. Until we break the mental bondage that inhibits so many of us, our thoughts will never rise above our basic expectations. The important point here is that you do not have to deny your ethnic background to become an expert at something other than sports or entertainment. You can be both.

College Graduates – Career Alternatives

GRADUATES MUST BE POSITIVE, PREPARED AND FLEXIBLE

The days when a college degree or job knowledge alone could bring advancement are gone forever. Too often we think a college degree is a super ticket; it is not. A degree is important, but it is no guarantee of success. Regardless of the high marks you earned in college, proving yourself in the real world is a challenge. It is a rare professor who dares to judge as harshly as an employer. Performance and work attitudes impact your compensation and career ascendancy.

It is my observation that college graduates have great difficulty overcoming the "school syndrome" once they have gravitated to the work force. Often it comes as a dreadful shock to discover that fellow employees (bosses, peers or associates) give direct instructions and criticize mediocre efforts. They expect others to nurture their hidden talents, gently guide them along, answer questions, make suggestions, or give constructive feedback. Students pay to be taught; employees are paid to learn on their own. They must learn their job duties, learn to increase their proficiency, learn about the company, learn to take responsibility, learn to observe and learn to broaden their business expertise.

In the business world, graduates will have to deal with rapid technological changes and increasingly intense competition at an accelerated, complex pace. In discussing technology and its effects on any phase of our lives, I could write for days and still not make a dent in the vast amount of knowledge humans have been accumulating and that continues to grow daily. The technological revolution we've been experiencing is aptly characterized as an explosion of information. New ideas, concepts and methods have given us products on Monday that become obsolete on Friday.

Tough economic conditions have led to corporate belt tightening and critical assessment of their personnel. I've walked the corporate tight rope and fortunate to have survived 9 reorganizations and downsizings in 6 years. I had to apply a growth formula that made every move I made appear to increase my value to the company. The challenge is to keep up with emerging technologies and remain competitive during this tidal wave of the ever-changing dynamics of today's business environment. Surviving and thriving in high-demand jobs depends, to a great degree, upon your balanced skill-set in getting the right things done – on time and with the desired results. Every day you will be judged on your ability to successfully manage multiple projects, competing priorities and critical deadlines.

Career Transitioners and Corporate Climbers
Master the Ten BE ATTITUDES

To effectively manage today's turbulent job market and to develop winning strategies in the career game, career transitioners and corporate climbers need to be aware of what I call the **"TEN BE-ATTITUDES." Don't overlook their fundamental importance in getting from the dorm room to the boardroom!**

◆ **BE FOCUSED** on the process of achieving your goals. Long-term thinking improves short-term and day-to-day decision making. Pay less attention to information that does not help you reach your goals. You can control your own mind chattering by eliminating distraction. When you get a distraction or destructive thought, slam the door. Someone who cannot control his thoughts is not free to direct his energies and will.

◆ **BE WILLING** to make sacrifices to reach long-term goals, and accept responsibility for your work actions. There is no substitute for hard work. Either you can do well in your job and work your way up, or you stagnate and rust your way out. Excuses for not taking action can torpedo your reputation and career. Put your attention on your intentions to cultivate a sense of urgency in your activities.

◆ **BE FLEXIBLE** and transfer existing skills and knowledge to new contents. The essential ingredient is to be prepared for changing employment caused by increased competition, new technology, resource overages or by changes in your value system. Job changes from downsizing, reengineering, mergers, acquisitions and reorganizations can be hard to face unless you convince yourself that you can handle them when they come. You should train yourself to react positively to change – to view it as an opportunity rather than a threat. Change is an opportunity for the individual who has learned how to learn in school and who does not take a narrow view of life. One of the hardest things to do is admit that we might be wrong. Admitting an error or mistake is the first step to positive change.

◆ **BE AWARE** of your company's internal political structure, office politics and power relationships. They are essential to getting ahead. The workplace is loaded with people engaged in power struggles. Marilyn Moates Kennedy, author of "*Powerbase: How To Build It, How To Keep It*," says, "If you are not aware of the politics in your office, you can jeopardize your career before you can catch on to the game." Further, she says "that politics and power building are never a substitute for doing the work well. They are complimentary, not competitive." "Knowledge makes you powerful because if you know about an opportunity or crisis in advance, you can figure out how it may affect you and you can plan a response. If you are not wired in, you simply react after the fact." Always keep your antenna tuned. Watch for warning signals at your company or within your industry that suggest your job is at risk.

◆ **BE AWARE** of corporate email lynching from fellow co-workers attempting to discredit you, question your work ethic or your decision making. Blind copies (bcc) are sent without your knowledge and contain the contents of your co-worker's email. Think before you decide to communicate your written response – it will see you through touchy situations. Learn to communicate effectively under pressure. Communicate the facts and address the issue in a professional, non-emotional tone.

◆ **BE CONCERNED** about setting priorities rather than budgeting time. One should plan daily activities based on their importance. This will allow you to focus on efforts, control events and find added hours in every day.

◆ **BE PREPARED** to negotiate a price for a new job, a promotion, or a competitive contract in terms of what you want and what the market will bear, instead of guessing. In negotiating, you have to walk in knowing your most important consideration. You have to know up front what you cannot afford to lose. Knowing how to get what you want, at the price you want and when you want it is probably the single most important set of skills there is for building your career and creating the lifestyle you want. Therefore, it stands to reason that if you improve your skills as a savvy negotiator, you can expect to achieve more wins and experience fewer losses.

◆ **BE PREPARED** to develop a strategy for a job search now, even if your job seems secure. Many job hunters postpone job screening until after they're fired. Today you need a "what-if" plan in place to cushion a financial set back. Work your business contacts while you are still employed.

◆ **BE AN AVID LISTENER**. Listen to understand others. Spend your energies asking questions rather than monopolizing the conversation. When you're talking, you're not listening. You can't overlook the results of failing to listen – wasted time, lost opportunities and strained relationships. Be quick to listen and slow to speak.

◆ **BE A PASSIONATE OBSERVER.** Observe people and events in your surrounding work environment with an unrelenting passion. It is the simplest, easiest way to dramatically reduce the amount of time it takes to learn how to achieve your goals. Observing others is your ultimate "secret" weapon.

◆ **BE THANKFUL** for problems. If they were less difficult, someone else with less ability might have your job. Keep an open mind when faced with difficult situations. You cannot control the tragic things that happen to you, but you can control your attitude and how you face up to them.

◆ **BE UNSELFISH AND SHARE** the positive attitudes and strong desire you have for education and achieving excellence to help develop other individuals who are not goal-oriented. Communicate this attitude and vision to them; it is a privilege to share. You should not get so busy that you neglect the responsibility of taking the things you have learned and feeding it back into the community. Your efforts to encourage your peers and the younger generation to pursue their educational endeavors will make an impact and, in turn, make a difference. Once you act upon this responsibility, you will prosper financially and spiritually in proportion to what you contributed.

Individually, these **BE-ATTITUDES** offer a rich source of insights to sharpening your business acumen and work place behaviors to reach higher levels of achievement in your professional and personal life. Whether you have just landed your first job or are going after a top position, these insights are priceless tools to charting a career and accelerating your success quotient in record time to become an asset to your company.

Career planning is part of life and educational development. Regardless of your major or year in college or whether you are job seeking or not, use every opportunity to network. If you narrow the job choices you are willing to investigate and pursue, you narrow the employment opportunities.

Please refer to Appendix 4 (page 105) for corresponding spiritual scriptures.

CHAPTER 5: KEEP YOUR MARKETING
OPTIONS AS WIDE AS YOUR INTEREST

Not very long ago, corporate recruiters did not recruit on HBCU campuses. Now, many perspective employers send recruiters to campuses to seek out and screen candidates. Today, the **COLLEGE CAREER CENTER** is the marketing center of the university. It is one of the most convenient, yet frequently overlooked sources of career assistance. College Career Centers act as a clearinghouse for information about the newest developments in areas of occupational interest, internships, résumé writing, testing, interview preparation and other relevant topics like counseling, computerized assessment and workshops.

The earlier students start utilizing this marketing gold mine, the better they will be prepared to face obstacles when entering the job market. There is a saying, "The difference between getting a terrific job or a terrific disappointment is the amount of preparation you invest into your development." Utilization of the College Career Center will improve your chances of finding job placement in a specific field.

I am definitely an advocate of student participation in College Career activities. This is an excellent area to expand your knowledge base, meet corporate representatives who can influence your career path and refine leadership skills. Student leadership and university organizations should take an active role in workshop participation and interaction with corporate representatives.

For example, students should serve as staff members or liaisons of the College Career Center. Students should work at the Career Planning and Placement Center to identify and distribute career information to the student populace to broaden their perspective toward the world of work. You should assist in the publicity of activities, programs and workshops/seminars sponsored by the College Career Center. Letters should be written to facilitate the acquisition of funds and support of specific college programs and activities from corporate America.

Equally important is the need for students to coordinate, implement and attend on-campus, student-oriented programs and activities. Some suggested college seminars/workshops to plan and initiate are:

- Employment Trends and Career Strategies for the New Millennium
- Tips for Success in the Business World
- The Corporate World – A Black Perspective
- Unwritten Rules of the Work Place
- Money Strategies: Tax, Investment Strategies and Using Other People's Money
- Careers in International Business – Opportunities in the Global Markets
- Entrepreneurship in Corporate America – Orientation Toward Business Formation
- Time Management and Positive Mental Attitude Breeds Success

- ◆ Graduate School vs. Entering the Work Force After Graduation
- ◆ Cultural Diversity in the Work Place

The Job Hunt

The biggest challenge for most diploma-seeking individuals is how to secure a job after graduation. It is hard, time-consuming work finding the job you want, and especially difficult seeking your first position. Today's changing and uncertain job market (corporate downsizing, stagnant raises, abrupt organizational changes, waves of corporate scandals and bankruptcies) makes that tough. At one time, men and women with specialized education and experience and proven accomplishments were in demand because demand outweighed supply. Now there are more people chasing fewer jobs. Making the transition from the academia halls to life after college isn't always an easy task.

Today's restructuring and still fragile economy has created a fluid job market and flexibility is at a premium. If you want to be employed, experts say, you must be willing to update your skills to maintain your marketability, be creative in your job search and be willing to move to new industries or even a new city. Change, flexibility and adaptability are the name of the game to navigate the constantly changing roller coaster of the real business world.

Job-hunting in today's market is not about throwing darts and hoping for a bulls-eye. Job-hunting in itself is a job and should be treated as such. It requires the same conscientiousness, discipline, consistency and time-spending as any other employment. If you are to be successful, you have to do something every day. And it's all tedious, time-consuming work – writing letters, following up, using your networking contacts, checking newspaper help-wanted ads, online career sites, and using the telephone and e-mail – two of the most important job-hunting tools at your disposal.

Job Hunting Tips

Final examinations may be over for college graduates, but the toughest questions are still ahead – in job interviews.

- ◆ Are you prepared to answer harder questions and provide figures to support your accomplishments?
- ◆ Are you prepared to verbalize the kinds of opportunity you seek in an interview? The grading is done by corporate recruiters who say they give high marks to rookies with intelligent questions of their own.

In simple terms, the kiss of death in an initial job interview can take many forms. Using a "what can you do for me" approach almost guarantees disappointment. Usually this statement or attitude is interpreted as a candidate's sole interest in what he will take from the company rather than what he intends to give. I remember in one of my first job interviews, I sabotaged my job-hunting efforts. I inquired about secondary issues like dental plans, vacations, lunch hours and parking recommendations. There's plenty of time to pursue these questions after a company has demonstrated an interest in making you an offer. The best recommendation I will make is to approach each interview as a difficult exam. Your A-plus performance might win a good job offer.

As one who has gone through the job-hunting process, sometimes being interviewed by a suit with no one in it and who promised things that never happen, I give you my sympathy.

It's often said that effective placement is being at the right place at the right time and being prepared. Apply these job-hunting tips for effective self-marketing to stay employed:

- The best time to start preparing for a job hunt is while you still have a job.
- The successful job hunter keeps trying and has a can-do attitude despite obstacles.
- Do your homework. Research organizations before you interview and present your unique qualifications for it. This shows initiative and interest. Preparation pays. Word of caution – communicate your qualifications without sounding superficial.
- Customize your job search to increase your chances of being selected. Launch a job campaign after mapping out your resources, tools and strategies. Target specific areas for interviews. Keep a contact list and results on log sheets. Pursue a number of job-hunting strategies at the same time to hedge against employment rejections.
- Determine your occupational and geographical limitations and flexibility. Ask yourself these three questions: Are you flexible in job descriptions? Are you willing to relocate or travel? Will you work nights or weekends?
- Use the on-line world as a career marketplace. Many employers invite the submission of on-line resumes.

◆ Dazzle them with a stellar resume that leaves a lasting impression. Remember, your resume is only a door opener. A personal interview is what you want. Jobs come through people, not paper.

◆ Don't rely on traditional employment agencies for help. Highly paid job opportunities are rarely advertised with them. You need interviews with decision makers with authority to create an opening.

◆ Avoid shot-gunning your cover letter and résumé to potential employers. An unsolicited résumé is just above advertising mail. A résumé is most effective when it's passed on by someone the person respects.

◆ Make sure your cover letter is brief, grammatically correct, succinct – and doesn't repeat what's on the résumé. Your cover letter is a prospective employer's first glimpse of writing skills. Articulate how your specific skills, experiences, education and volunteer work can benefit the company or a particular division, i.e. more sales revenue, better communications, or new product development.

◆ Try not to rely on recruiters. Informal networking is the best way to land a new job.

◆ Don't pre-screen a job out before your take the interview. Get as many job offers as you can. You can always turn down an offer, but you can't turn down a job if you don't have an offer.

◆ Define what you want and avoid the "What do you have – I'll do anything" myth. Employers prefer candidates with firm goals and objectives.

◆ Learn to respond appropriately and breathe your way through when asked difficult questions. What comes out of your mouth is as important as dressing for success and a first-class presentation.

◆ Don't take job rejections personally – it's a waste of time, talent and energy to fret over a job you did not get. Are you asking yourself, "I can't get a job because I need experience;" "I'm 1 of 100 applicants;" "There's too much competition;" "No one's hiring;" or "There must be something wrong with me." Avoid the tendency to blame yourself for failure. In many cases, it's not you but the supply and demand for the same position. In fact, the hiring decision may have more to do with office politics or other unknown situations you could not control.

◆ Follow-up on all applications. Always send a thank you note after each interview. After a few weeks, inquire about the status of your application or call to reaffirm your interest in the position. Employers admire persistence.

If you are really having a difficult time getting the job you want, consider moving to another area of the country where your skills may be in demand. A willingness to relocate broadens your job possibilities, not to mention the adventure of starting a new life.

Networking

You've got your degree. You're fired up with enthusiasm, and you've plunged into the job market with no luck. You are discouraged and beginning to doubt that you'll find a position in your chosen field. To make matters worse, those negative job market stories in the newspapers have really got you depressed.

Now what do you do? **NETWORK ... NETWORK ... NETWORK!!!**

First, let me tell you what networking is not. Some people think networking means calling friends and business acquaintances and asking them for a job. Instead, networking is like building a spider web. Contacts are made piece by piece until a job is caught. Contacts should be used to offer ideas, suggestions and names of executives with whom you can speak. Get in touch with them, ask for an appointment and pick their brains for ideas and additional contacts. Eventually, a solid job lead will appear.

Networking is necessary if you are going to make solid gains and advances in today's super competitive business world. In fact, many of the best jobs are never advertised to the general public. The greatest number of best jobs (at least 70%) are found in the unadvertised hidden market. Networking with business colleagues and other professional contacts is a valuable source of industry leads, salary levels within interested fields, career possibilities and identification of available employment positions. All of these contacts comprise an information system that you can easily tap to expand your networking base.

How To Network

Networking opportunities are everywhere for job seekers. Here is a compilation of techniques to improve your networking approach:

- ◆ It takes more than good luck, good looks and what you know to get the job you want. It is who you know and the referral network, or inner circle fraternity, who your contacts know. Your "networld" should consist of people who share common values, exchange support and help others create mutually beneficial opportunities.
- ◆ Network everywhere, all the time. Let everyone know who you are and what type of job you are seeking. Networking is low-cost advertising, especially if you expand your research to the Internet and libraries.
- ◆ Cultivate long-lasting, professional networking contacts to form powerful partnerships and alliances. Meeting someone is just part of the plan. Keep in touch with colleagues and external clients to stay in the information

loop. Maintaining contact keeps your name fresh in their minds.

◆ Continue expanding your circle of contacts by purposely seeking introductions that expose you to more job leads. Exchange business cards and explain what you do.

◆ Avoid doing business while networking. It is inappropriate and impractical. Make an appointment to meet your contact for lunch or for a drink.

◆ Act like a host, not a guest. Adele Scheele, author of Success Strategies, says guests wait to be introduced. A host introduces himself.

◆ One of my favorites – Give and Get. You cannot always be on the receiving end. Do favors. They are like a savings account. Someday you may want to draw on it.

◆ Edit your contacts. Eventually, you have to separate the productive from the non-productive. You cannot be involved with all of your contacts.

Are You A Rising Star?

Thriving in today's changing business trends, competitive challenges and shrinking job market, a fast tracker has to master the hidden code for success. A first-rate career plan and hard work may be the keys to career advancement, but in the corporate world, self-promotion is a valuable strategy to get where you want to go. If you don't advertise yourself to people, you could be a victim of what others plan for you, and that could be the start of career derailment. Assuming you have landed the first job, the first three months can make or break a promising career.

To help you ease into your new position, career experts suggest establishing a close relationship with a tenured co-worker who is well respected by peers. Ask potential mentors questions like, "What do I need to work on?" "What am I not doing enough?" "Where do I need experience I don't have?" "Are there others in the company I can talk to in the mentoring capacity?" Once you have identified a possible mentor, seek his or her advice. In *Getting Through To People*, Jesse Nirenberg wrote, "It means getting them to understand and agree with you. It means convincing your mentor your ideas, viewpoints, and beliefs are valuable. It means enlisting your mentor's full support." Remember, no mentor is going to protect you if your performance is not up to par. By mastering high-return tasks and expanding your job to embrace new goals, you boost the odds of getting noticed.

DO YOU CONSIDER YOURSELF A FAST TRACKER? ARE YOU A RISING STAR? Fast trackers advance within their companies because they know how to tap into critical resources. Slow trackers often aren't even aware these resources exist. Fast trackers don't necessarily attend better colleges. And the biggest surprise of all? They don't work any harder. They find ways to bring their excellent performance to their boss' attention. They know most people are busy worrying about their own successes and disappointments to be noticing them. Even your boss, who is paid to observe you, won't do it unless you find a way to get his attention. Learn how to get the word out about yourself … no matter what your endeavor!

You can be confident you are on the fast track if your boss:

- Provides you with special information that allows you to learn how the company really operates.
- Warns you about changes to be made within the organization.
- Assigns you challenging tasks.
- Advertises your strengths to higher management.
- Prepares you to handle more difficult assignments.
- Gives you enough authority to complete important assignments.
- Notifies you about promotion opportunities.
- Helps plan your long-range career.
- Warns you in advance – and in confidence – about your career problems.
- Asks for your input in decisions for which only the boss is responsible.

Zig Zigler, world renowned author of *See You At The Top*, says, "Your desire for achievement can be the most important tool in helping you reach your goals. Winners are people who take a little knowledge and turn it into a powerhouse of achievement." As you make career advancements utilizing your network channels, not only will you be writing new pages in history, you will also be creating opportunities for future alumni and other career-oriented students.

Stay Inspired, Committed and Determined To Create Amazing Results In Your Life. Ignite Your Creative Spark To Achieve Personal And Professional Excellence.

Please refer to Appendix 5 (page 108) for corresponding spiritual scriptures.

CHAPTER 6: TIME POWER – THE ART OF GETTING AHEAD

WHAT IS TIME MANAGEMENT? Time management is the foundation for everything you do in school, out of school, at work and in your personal life. It is the most precious and valuable resource you have. Simply … time management is self-management and it starts with established goals. Nothing is more convincing than the individual success you can experience from daily awareness of the importance of time! The great dividing line between success and failure can be expressed in five words, **"I Did Not Make Time."**

Time Doesn't Wait For Anyone Who Isn't Prepared! The way you prioritize your activities can save you considerable bother and expense as well as time. Learning to manage time properly is probably one of the most basic and critical skills you need to acquire to become an effective and well-prepared individual.

Profile of Time Wasters

Procrastinators are preoccupied with time. Whether or not you are a procrastinator yourself, it is important to examine the reasons that perpetuate why people put things off.

Here is one story about procrastination.
A painfully shy man fell in love with a young woman. He sensed that she felt the same way, but he couldn't find the courage to ask her out. Finally, he decided to mail her a love letter every day for one year and then ask her for a date. Faithfully, he followed his plan, and at year's end he was courageous enough to call her – only to discover she'd married the letter carrier.

This story emphasis how a few minutes can save a few hours.
There's a story about a man struggling to cut down enough trees to build a fence. An old farmer came by, watched for a while, then quietly said, "Saw's a kinda dull, isn't it?" "I reckon," said the fence builder. "Hadn't ya better sharpen it"? "Maybe later. I can't stop now – I got all these trees to cut down."

Ask yourself these questions. It is not necessary that you answer these questions in writing, just make a mental note of your response. Don't be surprised, disappointed and even offended if you answered "No" to many of these questions.

- Do you consider time a valuable asset?
- Do you often complain that you do not have enough time?
- Are you forever pulling yourself out of a one-time squeeze only to find yourself pressed immediately into the next?
- Do you have valid reasons for not doing more, or do you have excuses?

- How is it that some busy people never seem to have trouble finding the time needed to do the things they need to do while others can never find the time?
- Do you concentrate on daily objectives, focus your energy in the right places and eliminate wasted time and duplicated efforts?
- Do you think it is possible to organize your time, boost your efficiency and remember all the details of your busy day?
- Are you always putting things off – delaying everything until the very last minute?
- Are you disorganized and do you lack self-discipline?
- What will be your accomplishments in the next six months, year, two years? Would you like to surpass your earlier accomplishments and reach an even higher pinnacle of success?

THE EXCUSES START HERE ...

Nobody's nagging me, so I'll do it later.
It's too late to start this today.
I just didn't have enough time.
Not today. I have too much on my mind
Why do it now? It's not due yet.
If I finish this now, they'll just give me something else to do.
I meant to do it; I just forgot.
Next week – that's when I'll start my research paper.
Can't do it – can't make it – wish I could.
Out of the question – can't change – it's out of my hands.

AND END HERE!!

Attending classes	Studying for tests
Doing homework assignments	Writing papers
Keeping up with reading assignments	Talking with a teacher or advisor
Completing degree requirements	Taking oral or comprehensive exams
Balancing work with family time	Learning to delegate responsibilities

Change Your Time Wasting Behavior

Successful managerial skills are built on a firm foundation of time proven techniques to be more effective and accomplish more in less time. Time is both the driving force and the controlling influence in achieving your goals. In Willie Jolley's music and motivational power book titled, *It Only Takes*

A Minute To Change Your Life!, the author uses a quote from Dr. Benjamin Mays that says, "I have only just a minute – only 60 seconds in it. Forced upon me, can't refuse it, didn't seek it, didn't choose it, but it's up to me to use it. I must suffer it if I lose it, give account of it if I abuse it. Just a tiny little minute, but an eternity is in it."

The **Rules for Effective Time Management** below are provided to help you realize tremendous benefits from making time a part of your daily routine. **How much more effective and productive** could you become if you began to immediately apply some of these rules? **Use them NOW to change your time-wasting behavior** and to accomplish more in less time with less effort!

- ◈ **Leverage Your Time,** and you will begin to take charge of your life. You can only spend time; you cannot save it. It is not the amount of actual time – the hours and minutes you devote to your job. It's what you do with the time that counts. Crunch time by fitting activities you must do into shorter and shorter time slots. Don't squander the best times by doing routine jobs. Pick jobs or activities that match your readiness and high-energy levels. Try not to start a job before you think it through.
- ◈ **Plan Your Productivity. Take time – or make time – for things high on your priority list.** Focus on the most vital priorities, and take action to cause them to happen. As one self-improvement expert put it, "If you do not think you have time for it, you probably need it more than the rest of us." The way to stop the urgent things from getting in the way of the important things is to focus on objectives. Keep in mind, everything that is important doesn't have to be done right now – prioritize!
- ◈ **Manage Your Objectives and Results.** Refine your work by cutting unneeded steps out of every job. Examine your time-consuming routines. Ask yourself, "Why am I doing this?" "What would happen if I didn't do

it all?" and "What would happen if I did it differently?" Make it a goal to do whatever you do by intent, not as a reaction to others. Too often we lose sight of our objectives by getting bogged down with the process.

- **Practice the Power of TNT (today not tomorrow)** to cure the deadly habit of procrastination – the behavior of postponing or ducking the difficult problems. A prerequisite to success is refusing to do the unimportant. Procrastination prevents success and paves the way for failure. As one time expert said, "Procrastination is the destroyer of talent, the waster of energy, the drainer of ambition and the kiss of death to a promising career."

- **Learn to Delegate.** You can accomplish more if you don't try to do everything yourself. Differentiate between what you have to do yourself and what you can ask others to assist you with.

- **Excellence, Not Perfection** is the key to effective time management. Avoid the pitfall of perfectionism; it will paralyze you. Making an already excellent product perfect is a big time waster.

- **Draw a Picture or Diagram of the Issue** to get an understanding or agreement in less time. When explaining an idea that others do not understand, make comparisons.

- **Organize Your Time or Lose It**. If you do not have time to plan, you cannot work efficiently. Start the day off right – spend some time mapping out what you expect to accomplish. Get rid of your to-do list; instead, use an integrated, organized system to record all activities that need to be done or planned the day they need to be completed and in what priority.

- **Learn to Say NO**. It's always nice to help others, but avoid spending hours solving everyone's problems. Politely and firmly tell people you're busy, and call them back in a timely manner. Before you commit on the spot try saying, "I'd like to help you out but before I say yes, I

59

have to look at my calendar." Try working that caller ID and telephone screen to your advantage.

♦ **Organize Your Telephone Calls, Meetings, Paperwork and E-mails**. To control them, apply these principles to your everyday routine: **schedule** – establish time frames and frequencies for your activities and adhere to them; **plan** – think through in advance what and how you want to accomplish a task; and **eliminate** – avoid duplication and wasted effort. Apply the "do it, delegate it, refer it, toss it, file it" system to getting things done without wearing yourself down. With ineffective organization, you will find yourself drowning in a backlog of documents. Organizational problems are a matter of decision-making, not neatness.

♦ **Listening is One of the Most Effective Time-Management Tools**. Failing to listen will result in wasted time and lost opportunities.

♦ **Time is Money**. The dollar value of your time is costly. Learn to increase the value of each hour. Give yourself deadlines or a time limit to finish your project. For every appointment you make, budget for adequate time to travel and wait as well as cover for other minute wasters for the duration of the activity.

♦ **Choose a Challenging Pacesetter As a Point of Reference** for future performance or find an effective role model who demonstrates competent use of time. Plan schedules regularly with those who most directly influence what you do with your time.

COURAGE IS REQUIRED TO ELIMINATE THE BIG THREE PRODUCTIVITY KILLERS – Procrastination, Poor Planning and Personal Disorganization.

Success will elude you if you are a disorganized procrastinator who has no plan to gain control of your workday. You can have the brains and talent, a winning personality, creativity, great communication skills or financial wizardry but still need the courage to take appropriate actions for your life!

The next time you say, "I'm wasting time," change that to say, "I'm wasting myself." The value of your talents depends upon what you do with your time and how you prioritize your goals and objectives. Wasting time or losing time is a triple threat. Lost time means lost money, lost control and loss of confidence. Reducing or avoiding lost time is far more than just your time alone. And in business, timing is everything.

> **We face no greater challenge in our personal and professional lives than organizing our daily activities and activities and managing our time effectively.**

Please refer to Appendix 6 (page 111) for corresponding spiritual scriptures.

CHAPTER 7: PLAN TODAY OR PAY TOMORROW

Now that you are on the receiving end of a regular paycheck, I welcome you to the working world and to the wonderful world of taxes. Without a knowledge of how the financial universe operates and how you can tap into it, you will feel helpless and without power. Navigating the maze of all things financial can be a daunting, confusing journey.

It is more important than ever to understand the choices available to you – and to determine what's right for you. No longer is it good enough to have your head above water – you have to start swimming toward a goal. Whatever your situation – and whatever your income – there are steps you can take to get your money under control and to start making better-informed, educated financial decisions. This is why you need a money management system that defines your goals, creates a plan to achieve them and stretches your dollars to cope with financial problems that might arise unexpectedly.

Managing Your Finances Wisely

Let's talk about money – specifically your money and how to manage the financial transactions in your life. If you are really satisfied with your financial astuteness, you need not read on. But if you are like most of us who are struggling to execute a budget, the answer is a resounding NO!

We all know people who have high-paying jobs or operate their own business, yet never seem to have enough money. There are only a few who are exempt from the pressures of balancing a checkbook and presenting a positive cash flow. Others, even though they earn far less, manage to accumulate enough wealth over the years to live comfortably and retire with security. What makes this difference? Is it personal cash management, financial planning, good credit, accurate record-keeping, financial positioning, tax reductions or other financial disciplines? This is what Chapter 7 will talk about – our money and money management!

Today we must plan our finances in a new and uncertain, unpredictable economic climate. The financial marketplace is more complicated than ever before, but the fundamentals of good money management remain the same. Don't let the disquieting uncertainties of today's economy lure you into taking a "wait and see" approach. You still have personal goals to meet and choices about how to meet them. In fact, your best defense during insecure times can be a plan for making the most of the money you have so you're prepared for whatever the economy hands you.

Financial Planning to Handle
Life's Financial Surprises

The reason I'm a strong advocate of financial planning is that for several years I had no financial plan to achieve either short, medium – or long-term goals. At the age of 29, I resigned my position as a US Air Force commissioned officer for a marketing vice president position with a promising company in the lucrative mortgage banking and insurance industry. In this business venture, I was on target to live comfortably and retire in years, not decades with long-term, walk-away residual income from repeat business and investments. Then **POOF** ... my bright future was vanishing right before my eyes and I became helpless. The company treaded into diversification areas within multiple industries before the infrastructure was in place to withstand the fickle capital markets. Operating dollars were minimal to develop proprietary software needed to brand and expand the business.

As a result, my attention got distracted. My confidence waned. My motivation slipped away and was in a downward spiral. I was like a boat without an anchor – drifting aimlessly and endlessly. My pride got in between past achievements and present shortcomings. I experienced strong pangs of guilt. I became not only financially bankrupt but also mentally and psychologically bankrupt. I was caught up in a financial hurricane and became entrapped in a poverty mentality and negative attitudes. Personally, I was ignorantly cooperating in my own failure by failing to turn adversity into motivation.

I'm sharing this because it does not matter whether you fail or succeed. What matters is how you perceive your financial situation and how you react to it. Wealth is a characteristic of thought. I perceived my outcome a failure and this attitude paralyzed any steps I took to get out of the quicksand. In that stage of my life, I ended up accomplishing **NOTHING** and losing **EVERYTHING** of material value – car repossession, home foreclosure, cashed-out stocks and liquidation of other assets I owned - but my inner spirit was strengthened to endure the uphill journey. I not only became a more humble person, I developed an attitude of gratitude for people and the few materialistic items that remained in my life! My spirit now soars with positive momentum, and I am attracting opportunities which are in harmony with my vision. Each day is an opportunity to maximize the moment with consistency of effort and a cheerful countenance.

Before I go any further, let me tell you what financial planning is and why it's very important. The purpose of financial planning is to improve the quality of life – to live and love better. It is a tool and organized process to help you enjoy not just the future but the past as well. The key to a workable money management plan is planning. It is the continuing process of defining on paper:

- ◆ Where are you financially?
- ◆ What specific long-range financial goals do you want to achieve?
- ◆ What is the best way to achieve your goals?

- ◆ What is your plan for day-to-day, week-to-week, or month-to-month spending?
- ◆ Would you like to reduce your debt or increase your savings?
- ◆ What is your plan for accumulating financial resources for emergencies and long-range financial security?

Achieving financial goals you establish for yourself often means making a whole new series of decisions. Only you can **TAKE CHARGE** (two of the most important words in building personal wealth) of your financial situation to control your financial future. Understanding your cash flow, investigating new financial options and injecting a strong dose of discipline will help you forge a path to real financial independence. For those of you who until now have lived without the advantage of clearly defined financial goals, financial planning will give you new confidence.

Once you have agreed on your financial priorities, you are literally one step closer to your desirable goals of financial security. However, keep in mind your job is not finished. Financial security isn't something that happens automatically. As your circumstances change, your money management plan will have to change too.

Be prepared to review your plans at least annually or even every 6 months and adapt them as you see fit. Your blueprint for money management will look different from anyone else's plan because it must originate with your list of goals, your timetable for achieving them and your choices for how to achieve them. As you work through your personal money management planning, you will learn much about where you are and where you want to go financially. But understanding your financial circumstances more clearly is only a beginning point. Whether your need is security, savings, investment or another financial service, you should begin your planning at whatever stage of life you find yourself right now. I purposely said stage of life instead of age because these days, age is no longer a sure marker of when people finish school, marry, have children or even retire.

Personal Cash Management – the Simple Way to Financially Succeed

Quote: "The easiest job I have ever tackled is that of making money. It is, in fact, almost as easy as losing it." (H.L. Menchen)

Most people feel – no matter what their income – that they need more money to meet their expenses. I certainly did after experiencing career anxiety, career stagnation and tough times. I had to learn how to better manage my finances and seriously adjust my attitude towards money. Every aspect of my life – my career, marriage and even happiness – was impacted by my lack of monetary control. Experience has shown me that in our inflationary economy, more money is not always the answer to obtaining financial stability and security. Don't get me wrong; earning more money is nice, but what really counts is how much you keep and what you do with it. What is often just as important in determining our financial goals is how we plan and spend our money.

I remember reading an article in *Black Enterprise*, written by its CEO, founder and publisher Earl G. Graves Sr., who said, "In personal money management, as in business, the issue is not just income but ownership. Putting a value on disciplined saving and goal-oriented investing is equally as important as career success and entrepreneurial achievement." Your portfolio begins with savings – the starting point of your wealth-building journey. No matter which way you look at it, money saved is money earned, and this is the prime source of the best money-saving, money-making information available. Treat your savings as a billed expense, actually paying yourself first. Most importantly, regard that savings as untouchable.

It is important to remember that good money management starts long before you begin keeping track of the dollars and cents. A good money-management strategy begins with your dreams. Write them down. Opposite each item, quantify them with a time frame and a dollar amount. Next, consider the best ways to enact your financial goals. Since your money plan is a personal or a family matter, you need to take a good look at your values, at your goals that reflect these values, and all the resources you have available to you. Your major financial decisions – the best time to buy a house, the type of credit to use, the best investments to choose – will always be affected by your stage in life as well as economic conditions.

A financial plan that does not match your money personality is going to frustrate you and ultimately fail. It is not necessary to change your personality, only to recognize it and put your specific traits to use. Start by taking inventory of your investing personality, asking:

- Am I a hands-on operator who demands control of his destiny?
- Am I the easy-going type who'd rather not get involved in the nuts and bolts of financial management and investing?
- Do I have the intestinal fortitude to withstand another point plunge in the market? Do I have the patience and enough fall-back money to wait for the outcome?

Finally, remember that good money management is more than a mathematical formula. It's too closely tied to the ups and down of living for that. Your money plan is always subject to change if your life situation changes. The object of a good budget is to make your money help you reach your goals, not to compel you to conform to rigid spending rules.

Once you have a good idea where you're going, you need to figure out from where you're starting. To help you assess what resources you have, you'll need to figure out your personal net worth – a snapshot of your current financial statement status. Your net worth is an account of everything you own minus everything you owe. It's as valuable to you as any bottom-line statement is to the president of a company. Net worth will tell you how much money you actually have, how much is tied up in debt, how much can be earmarked for your goals and whether any of it could be earning more for you elsewhere.

Earl G. Graves, Sr. also said, "If you have access to a company-sponsored 401(K) investment savings program, you can get into the market without the expense and risk of investing in individual stocks. When it comes to saving money, the future is now."

When it comes to choosing investments, the best ones are those that truly reflect your goals, dreams, tolerance for risk and your financial personality. The amount you begin to invest is not nearly as important as getting into the investment habit. Small, consistent investments become giants in time. One of the best secrets of any sound financial plan is to avoid putting all your eggs in one basket; spread the wealth by creating a portfolio that includes a blend of financial products. Different investments react differently to the same market conditions, so it's essential to hedge your bets.

To create a diversified portfolio:

- Determine whether you want investments with the potential to generate income, capital or both.
- Decide how long you'll keep your money invested.
- Consider how much risk you can tolerate.
- Ensure you have proper protection to replace your income and protect your assets.
- Stick with your plan.

Your portfolio is like a puzzle fitting together to meet your investment needs. By diversifying, you automatically reduce the risk inherent in any form of investing. Just make sure that your portfolio is diversified well enough so that you can afford an occasional mistake.

Credit Profile
– Best Indicator Of Financial Health

I think the responsible use of credit is one of today's greatest challenges. Your credit profile literally affects everything you do; therefore, there is a need to nurture a good credit rating and profile. With almost every important financial move and employment hiring opportunity, a credit inquiry and credit report from one of the three national credit agencies is involved.

In protecting your credit, you should use your credit wisely to cautiously and faithfully meet your financial obligations. It is very important that your debt repayment habits reflect prudence and timeliness. By fulfilling your obligations, you will establish a firm financial foundation for you and your credit. Over-extensions can lead to credit trouble. If you use credit to buy more than you can afford, you are inviting problems that may last for years.

CREDIT CARD CAUTION FOR COLLEGIANS

Credit, in the form of student loans, may have made it possible for you to attend college. Now that you have graduated, credit can continue to play a role in your life. A defaulted student loan can scar your credit for years. While you have the right to use credit made available to you, the obligation exists to use it wisely.

71

THESE 6 C's COUNT FOR CREDIT

Character	– a sincere attitude toward paying your bills.
Capacity	– ability to repay loans from money coming in.
Capital	– owning property or things worth more than your debt.
Conditions	– agreements made in advance between lender and person borrowing.
Collateral	– possessions which are set aside for deposits as security for the debt.
Common Sense	– ability to use credit wisely.

PLASTIC MANIA AND DEBT TRAPS

To the vulnerable or the uninitiated, credit looks like "free money." A $3,000 credit limit means $3,000 floating adrift in the financial universe. With the American Dream soaring beyond most people's income, it's only too tempting to take that fatal bite of the credit apple. And woe unto you afterward (and I'm speaking from experience), you'll be paying for that lunch you couldn't afford yesterday – but charged anyway – for many tomorrows to come.

Putting your head and wallet together with a few pointers, can mean a prosperous relationship in using your credit wisely. Build and protect your credit rating by taking advantage of these credit tips:

◆ Streamline credit card spending so every dollar is put to its best use. Prepare a monthly budget and compare your expenses with your income to determine how much debt you can afford to assume.
◆ Revolving high-interest credit card debt is one of the worst kinds of debt. By consistently carrying high-

interest credit card debt, you are creating a scenario that can grow quickly into an unhealthy financial situation.

◆ Manage your credit balances and pay on time to avoid monthly fees. You can now use a personal computer and modem to manage all of your financial affairs – bank accounts, credit cards, monthly bills, investments, retirement funds, etc.

◆ The best way to build your credit is to use it – but wisely. Avoid reaching your credit limit in order to save on finance charges and have credit available for emergencies. Making regular payments on a timely basis will help improve your credit rating.

◆ Financial experts generally recommend keeping personal debt (including rent/mortgage) at or below 40% of monthly take-home pay.

◆ Try to avoid the minimum payment trap, and try to increase the amount you pay down each month, even a little, to bring down the interest. While these smaller payments seem to allow you to hold onto more cash each month, they really add up to major expenses.

◆ Avoid doing business with companies that shotgun your credit requests to multiple vendors. Frequent credit inquires will negatively affect your favorable credit ratings.

◆ Check for inaccuracies on your credit report to monitor possible credit fraud or identity theft at least twice a year or before major purchases. Be sure to examine your files from all three national credit reporting agencies as the information may not be the same on each one. If you find errors, take steps to dispute the information in order to have it removed from your file. If you have been refused credit within the past 30 days and the reason for the rejection was an unfavorable credit report, you have the right to know which credit agency was used to obtain the report. You have the right to dispute any and all derogatory and negative information about you, which may be making it difficult or impossible to obtain credit, insurance or employment. You have the right to demand the credit bureau send corrected copies of your report to all creditors who received the incorrect reports for the LAST 6 MONTHS. The credit bureaus will only do this when you ask.

◆ If you share a joint credit account, be sure the account is reflected on both credit reports. This will ensure separate credit identities for each cardholder or signee.

DETERMINE YOUR DEBT LOAD

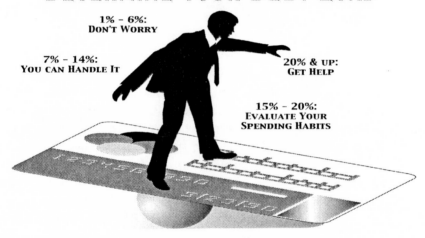

1% – 6%:
DON'T WORRY

7% – 14%:
YOU CAN HANDLE IT

20% & UP:
GET HELP

15% – 20%:
EVALUATE YOUR
SPENDING HABITS

The Ultimate Career Security Is Financial Security.

The keystone of career security in this new employment world is a money strategy that will give you the support and the flexibility you need, no matter what direction you want your career to take. First, you will need to broaden your financial base so that you are less dependent on a single employer. Second, take the financial steps that will allow you the option of going out on your own in the business world without money worries.

Through the years, I have learned that **financial independence is not measured by a certain amount of money**. **Being financially free** means having just the right amount, based on the lifestyle you desire, to be able to freely choose what you want to do each and every day. The **essence of wealth accumulation** is directly tied to self-discipline that demands an automatic, systematic will to achieve financial goals.

To change my financial portfolio, I applied these sound financial principles to get predictable results and increase my future purchasing power:

- **Put Your Financial Goals in Writing**. You cannot continue to just dream about your financial goals. Write down specific goals to serve as a reminder and chart them as you progress.
- **Create A Simple Record-Keeping System**. The first fundamental aspect of mastering your finances is getting organized. Record-keeping is a matter of understanding what it is that you need to keep and having one centralized place to put everything. You need record-keeping (i.e., balancing your checkbook regularly) to gain control of your financial life and to track progress toward financial goals. Pay attention to where you spend your money.
- **Maximize Your Earning Power to Obtain Financial Fitness**. Whether by choice or by chance, it is imperative to make the most of today while planning for tomorrow. Become increasingly savvy about managing your hard earned income. Grow and maximize your assets to increase your earning power and to build wealth. Measure your personal wealth by net worth, not income. Wealth is what you own; income is what you annually earn.
- **Save Your Way to Wealth**. A wise man once said, "It is not what you earn, it is how much you consistently save

75

and invest on a regular basis." Stop the cash hemorrhaging by plugging the big money drains that absorb a lot of your money. Go on a strict "crash" money diet to get back in control of your troubled personal budget. Pay yourself first – the 10% to Wealth approach. Starting with your next paycheck, take 10%-15% of your after-tax income and place it in a high-yield, separate savings account, money market fund, or your company 401K allocation plan using pre-tax dollars.

◆ **Eliminate Debt Using the Debt-Reduction Pyramid Method.** Prioritize the bills to pay off first, then the next and so on. Write down all outstanding credit card balances in ascending order (smallest to largest). Focus on completely paying off the lowest balance. Paying off the lowest credit card balance eliminates the top of the debt pyramid. If the minimum monthly payment is $40 on the smallest balance, a check could be written for $75 ($40 minimum required plus an additional $35). Pay this extra amount every month until the entire balance of the first card is paid off. Once the lowest card is completely paid off, concentrate on the second position. Add the minimum monthly payment of the first card to the minimum monthly payment of the second smallest credit card. For example, if the minimum payment on the first card is $40 and the payment for the second card is $55, then your monthly payment to the second credit card would be $95 ($40 +$55 = $95). The benefit of using this step is that the minimum payments are already allocated in your budget. Thus, no additional money is reallocated to pay off outstanding debt. Continue using this strategy until all credit cards are completely paid off.

◆ **Use Credit Sensibly - Avoid Dumb Debt.** Credit can be a tool for cash management if used wisely for things you need and can afford. Smart spending can be a path to financial success. However, there are times when you borrow or buy an item on credit because it's an emergency and you worry about repayment later. Let's face it, not every use of credit is smart debt. Smart debt is borrowing money to make more money. The simple point is ... use credit only for the right reasons, not because you don't have money in your checking account. Use every dollar you're wasting on dumb debt toward building your wealth.

◆ **Reduce Your Tax Liability To Make Your Life Less Taxing**. Income taxes are the biggest expense you will encounter in life. Look at reducing your tax liability as a means of increasing your cash flow. Tax-smart strategies are actions to automatically and legally qualify you for additional deductions to keep more of your hard-earned dollars. Creating a good tax plan is essential to eliminating tax liabilities or deferring payment of taxes you pay on income. The secret to paying fewer taxes is to rearrange your financial affairs to avoid paying unnecessary taxes. In other words, make the money you spend tax deductible as you spend it. One example is to increase your take-home pay by changing your withholding. Use it to pay off debt. If your annual IRS refund is $600, you should stop overpaying the IRS and use the $50 a month you added to your paycheck to pay off debts, or invest the money and watch it grow. Let your money make money for you.

◆ **Educate Yourself on Different Investment Concepts and Vehicles That Impact Your Portfolio.** There's an almost infinite venue of investment vehicles that can make your hard-earned money grow. The fundamental tenet of successful investment is knowing what you're getting into and what you hope to achieve. Informed investors no longer can throw money in stocks and sit back counting their returns. The "buy and forget" investment strategy days are gone. If money is limited, develop a winning proposal and presentation – use "Other People's Money" (OPM) to create wealth. It takes access to money to make money.

◆ **Think Beyond Your Single-Source Paycheck**. Wage income is not enough; you need multiple income streams flowing into your bank account for financial freedom! The overwhelming majority of jobs are becoming less stable, less lucrative and less available. Increasingly, jobs are here today and gone tomorrow. This means the vast majority of wage earners are just one to three missed paychecks away from poverty. This does not necessarily mean you have to abandon the traditional corporate structure to become an independent business owner. You can find a rewarding part-time job to explore as a career alternative. You can acquire home ownership or investment property to generate rental income or start a part-time business to generate profit income and tax deductions –or at least invest to create income producing assets so that you can live off the interest. This could come from the royalties of a book, patent of a clever new gadget or the right investment choice that makes money for you while you sleep.

SPECIAL NOTE: The author is not engaged in rendering financial or tax services to the reader through the sale of this book. It only gives you an insight to important matters concerning your financial positioning. Since individual financial situations do vary, the reader should consult a competent professional on questions specific to financial or tax-related investment decisions.

Have You Achieved the Goals Of Wealth Creation and Wealth Preservation?

Plan For Tomorrow By Knowing Where Your Money Is Spent Today. Implement Money Management Strategies To Build Leverage Into Money-Making Activities!

Please refer to Appendix 7 (page 114) for corresponding spiritual scriptures.

CHAPTER 8: IT'S YOUR FUTURE. PLAN AND CREATE IT!

This book offers ways to increase your desire and motivation for academic excellence, career accomplishments and improved business acumen. There is no magic in these pages. They have just provided insightful ideas to make your learning shorter, easier and a lot less painful. As you read this book, the message is clear: **"If You Lose Sight of Time and Opportunity Before You, the Future Will Ignore You."**

What are you going to do with your future? The power of choice is yours to create a positive and productive plan for your life. Each day represents an opportunity to turn ordinary moments into extraordinary events or activities. Each day, each hour, and each minute are special and can be filled with accomplishments. Live your life with persistent determination to achieve greater and greater accomplishments.

Awaken the Winner Within

I see a world that is familiar with the words "no," "maybe," "I do not know," "someday," "one day," "never," "always" and "I cannot." These words indicate a self-limiting behavior and negatively influence our thought patterns. We should eliminate these words from our mental dictionaries and spoken vocabularies and instead, choose words that support a prosperous future. **More ideas and aspirations have gone down to failure on the word "IF" than perhaps any other word. It is time we recognize and defeat the three L's that ruin the lives of so many people – Lack, Limitation and Loss.**

Let these questions permeate your mind. Their answers will fuel your desire to achieve more or cause you to settle for less than your **TRUE** potential.

- Are you **open to new ideas and want to improve**?
- Are you **willing to live creatively, enthusiastically and proudly**?
- Are you an **enthusiastic minded individual who refuses to accept the word failure**?
- Are you an individual with a **positive attitude who has a VOCABULARY OF SUCCESS**?
- Are you a **winner who uses failure as a stepping stone to ACHIEVE YOUR ULTIMATE AMBITION**?
- Will your success journey be without **SELF-IMPOSED BOUNDARIES AND LIMITATIONS**?
- Do you have a "**CAN DO**" attitude toward life, work ethics, and everyday situations?

As you read through the questions did any of them describe you? It goes without saying ... **Attitude shapes your life and is everything that happens to you, around you or within you**. Attitude is paramount in achieving personal fulfillment. Give each letter of the alphabet a number: a=1, b=2, c=3, etc. If you add up the letters of the alphabet in the word, "Attitude," this is the result:

A	=	1
T	=	20
T	=	20
I	=	9
T	=	20
U	=	21
D	=	4
E	=	5

Attitude is 100%.

I see a world that refuses to recognize and encourage the smallest amount of human potential; however, our minds were meant to be creative and productive. Thoughts determine what you want. Actions determine what you get. Every person has a dream – a heart's desire, passion, a vision in their life that empowers their belief system and mental attitude. The doorway to creating positive changes in your life is finding your purpose in life, which ultimately drives your dreams and ambitions to shining realities. What are you waiting on?

ARE YOU PAYING ATTENTION? IT'S TIME TO WAKE UP!

I see a world that does not have a heart of passion. Can't you sense the urgency to spread love and kindness abroad? We need to release the priceless gift of love from within and it will transcend our egotistical mindset and selfish attitudes! Feel the love that you are, embrace it and become it in every way. As you allow this love to come forth, you experience the essence of life. Learn to love in deed and in truth and not merely talk about it.

I see a world that does not hear the cries of the unfortunate, poor, sick and needy. It is sad so many people cannot hear the begging and pleading because they are so trapped into their own misfortunes. Why is this? Is it possible we have become conditioned to ignoring the application of unity, diversity and equality in our lives? Are we one solid chain of peace, happiness, sharing and caring, or is it each of us is the missing link because our efforts are focused on building blocks and individual differences between us? No individual, company or world race can survive if we do not work in harmony, respect diversity, embrace individual differences and welcome new perspectives.

I see a world whose hands refuse to shape and illustrate to the young generation how things are and how they could be. Role models and mentors are difficult to find and seldom embrace their full potential. Never compromise who you are personally for who you aspire to be professionally. Who we are is more valuable than what we do. Our worth as a person is not based on our intelligence, our grades or how hard we work. It's our disposition and not our position that defines who we are. Rather than walk this earth lightly, role models and mentors should walk firmly with fierce determination and leave their marks. What you put back into the lives of others comes back into your own. So lead by example and with integrity, not only in business and your career, but also in your daily activities. Future generations depend on our efforts and our attitude of gratitude.

Finally, **I BELIEVE IT IS URGENT** that **WE**, the **LEADERS OF OUR GENERATION**, realize the dynamic power we possess to embrace devastating issues facing this generation. Imagine the impact of our combined strength and unselfish, individualized efforts. We represent a strong economic, social and political force to develop positive and effective solutions to unite, educate and economically empower those less fortunate. Equally as important, we should believe in our goals together and work toward our goals together, and we will undoubtedly achieve our goals together. We should focus and place our energies on investing our minds, abilities, talents and time to reach an abundant return. By uniting and flexing our collective muscles, we can increase our self-worth, our economic self-sufficiency and look upon ourselves as builders, thinkers and producers. We must avail ourselves for this cause and exemplify the strength of unity with purpose.

Hard Work + No Purpose = Wasted Energy

As a student of life, you have to seize the opportunity and embrace it where you are in relationship to your goals and priorities. This principle will help you confront educational challenges, and surprisingly, you will find the world awaits your enthusiasm and persistence.

Individuals who recognize that their minds were meant to be creative and productive can become their visions. We simply have to realize and truly grasp an awareness of who we are and our true potential. The challenge is to take off our masks and get in touch with our true selves. It's deciding what you really want, not what you think you want, not what someone else wants you to want – but what you want deep down.

For this reason alone, it is our responsibility to stand up, be counted and be willing participants in nurturing the seeds of greatness within us. It is always better to take action rather than to keep your feet firmly planted in "Nowhereville." Each of us has the potential to make an impact and enrich the world though our individual efforts.

Try avoiding this big mistake. Many times we are our own biggest enemy, and this closes many doors of opportunity in our path. We need to realize that an opportunity is only an opportunity if it's recognized and seized. When opportunity knocks at your door, be prepared to provide assistance. Your own efforts might be enhanced by those same knocks of opportunity.

Our society provides us with many avenues to improve our financial status and obtain incredible success in all aspects of our life. Each of us has the will to achieve our goals, dreams, and passions. It does not matter if you are from an affluent family, an economically depressed family or somewhere in between; you are accountable for your own success or failure. Inherently, each of us has the abilities and innate qualities to rise above the ordinary and commonplace. In the final analysis, each of us is in the business of building our lives with integrity and passion, regardless of who signs our check.

- What will be your legacy?
- Will you make integrity your trademark?
- Will you become the individual you know you can become and should become?
- Will you live and leave a legacy that will transcend your lifetime?

You see, life is like a baseball game. You have to step up to the plate and focus on the pitch coming toward you. You may hit a single, double, triple or even a grand slam. Many people fail because they fail to implement the golden rule of applying **FOCUS, FOLLOW THROUGH** and **FAITH** to hit the ball or to move their thoughts into action. **Focus** is zeroing in like a laser beam with enthusiasm to give power to your purpose. **Follow-through** is consistent implementation of productive thoughts and actions. And lastly, **Faith** is belief in accomplishing your goals with definition of purpose and conviction.

The Best Way to Predict Your Future Is To Create It.
A Vision + NO Work = Dream Deferred.

My desire is that you see your purpose driven life filled with promise and opportunity. Discover your responsibilities, challenge your thoughts and then develop them to create the life you deserve. Resolve today that you will accept nothing less than the best for yourself and accept life challenges. More importantly, I urge you to take charge of your activities and your efforts will turn stumbling blocks into building blocks - transforming challenges into triumphs.

Every effort should be made to concentrate on what you want to be, and that is what you will become. This truly is only the beginning for you, and a good beginning is measured by the journey it takes to get a greater sense of purpose and direction. Along this journey, you will learn valuable lessons about your life assignment. Enjoy what you choose to do and demonstrate a fierce desire for hard work.

The future indeed belongs to those who obtain a good education (on-the-job or hard knocks) and who prepare for future employment needs by learning new skills. As time continues to tick away, it brings you closer to whether success or failure is written by your name. This ticking away is your life span. Do not be haunted by missed opportunities and "what ifs." **It's time to leverage your hard work and create your future. It's time to live your dreams, walk in your purpose and make a mark on society. It's time to apply your talents and abilities to turn the power of your thoughts into measurable advancement of your goals. Now is the time to energize your ambitions and charge up your Belief in Yourself**!

Empowerment specialist Arthur L. Andrews in *Maximize Your Potential* spoke these powerful and dynamic words. Repeat them to improve your mental disposition and will to act.

"I am on this planet for a purpose and I realize that I must fulfill that purpose.
I step forward boldly to claim my birthright.
I take full responsibility for my life right now.
I am a worthy human being and I deserve the best.
I know what I am focused on will expand in my life.
The mark of greatness is truly upon me."

Go after your dreams to bring greater meaning, purpose and achievement in your life. Find your mountain, climb it and you will find your destiny! Don't stop reaching for the top. Stay hungry! Stay humble! Stay helpful! Stay motivated! Harness your potential to enrich the world! No matter what ... believe you can and you will!

Lastly, choose today to maximize your potential embracing each moment with enthusiasm, creativity, integrity and a cheerful countenance. Demand of yourself immediate, intelligent, persistent and consistent action toward the attainment of all goals. Choose today to make the impossible happen because you are standing at the brink of incredible life fulfillment.

Only those who risk going too far will ever know
how far they can go. Your OUTCOME in life
does not depend on your INCOME but rather on
your ability to OVERCOME. A Dream With
ACTIVITY Becomes REALITY!!!

**Please refer to Appendix 8 (page 119) for corresponding
spiritual Values.**

 **INTRODUCTION TO SPIRITUAL VALUES**

Unless noted, all scripture references are from the Holy Bible, New International Version by International Bible Society.

It is with gratitude and humility that I write this section of the book. I am not apologetic when speaking about my spiritual awakening and new understanding. My sincere desire is that this reading will prove edifying and encouraging to everyone who reads it and that it will strengthen their faith and walk in the messiah, our Father of creation and life. We are admonished to be deeply rooted and well founded spiritually. Explore the following pages to provoke your thinking, spiritual growth and maturity for the "Renewing of your Mind".

The Bible is the least understood and the world's bestselling book, and yet, it is the book that almost nobody knows! It often gets dusty, and like the human mind, it is not put to its full potential. The Bible, a corrective and directive book for all mankind, can give you peace, happiness and self-control when it is understood. Within it are answers to hidden esoteric mysteries.

No matter who you are, there is clear and irrefutable evidence in science, mathematics, anatomy, historical events, and fulfillment of prophecies to prove our Heavenly Father's existence is real, and the Bible is an expression of written words to mankind. Everyone – seekers, doubters, fervent believers, Bible students, ministry and scholarly leaders.

The **Bible is like a jigsaw puzzle**. All the pieces are there, but before the complete picture can be seen, the pieces have to be put accurately together. Those pieces only go together one way and then the true picture emerges. The Bible is just like the emerging picture, and **John 14:6** says there is one truth and one way. The challenge is finding and embracing universal, infallible truth in an age of deception and spiritual warfare. Yearning for higher spiritual understanding according to accurate knowledge must be top priority. Often times we error from habit, ignorance or disobedience.

- ◆ How long will it be before we see the true light of the world because our works were evil? **Titus 1:16** says "they claim to know God, but by their actions in works they deny Him." In **2 Timothy 3:5** it says "having a form of godliness but denying the power thereof."
- ◆ How long will we walk in darkness and be in bondage to Satan and his ministers operating the Mystery of Iniquity?

If we knew we were deceived, there would be no deception. Is this why we continue to act and behave as we do completely oblivious of the peril that is forth coming and eternal damnation that awaits us? The following quote from **Matthew 7:13-14** is sound admonishment: "Enter through the narrow gate. For wide is the gate and broad is the road that leads to destruction, and many enter through it. But small is the gate and narrow the road that leads to life, and only a few find it."

A **Divine pattern was shown to Moses** while atop Mt. Sinai **(Exodus 24)**, and it explains our Heavenly Father's **PURPOSE, PATTERN AND PLAN**. It is stipulated in everyone's Bible (regardless of translation) and is found in **Exodus 25:8-9, Exodus 25:40** and **Hebrews 8:5**. This divine pattern is imprinted on all life – the human body, atoms, space, etc., and unravels His eternal make-up. This same pattern is the universal spiritual law that controls the operations of the revolving nine planets with an unerring accuracy.

Our Heavenly Father reflects himself in all HIS creation (animate and inanimate, visible and invisible) because He is the

Archetype (Original) pattern of the universe. HIS glory permeates all things **(John 1:1-4; Colossians 1:15-18)**. He is the Father, Word and Holy Spirit, and they agree as One **(1 John 5:7-9)**.

For example:

- ◆ **Mosaic Tabernacle** in the Old Testament was built with three levels – Most Holy Place, Holy Place and Court Round About. **Three levels but One Tabernacle**. **Hebrews 8:5** says, "this tabernacle was an example and shadow of heavenly things."
- ◆ **Solomon Temple** was built with three levels – Porch, Sanctuary and Oracle. **Three levels but One Temple.**
- ◆ **Man and Woman are made with a three-fold physiological make-up;** a body, soul and spirit or soma, psyche and pneuma. **Three-fold but One Individual**.
- ◆ **Atoms** – the smallest particle known to the scientific world – have a Proton, Neutron and Electron. **Three-fold but One Atom**.
- ◆ **Living Cells** in plants or animals – the smallest unit of life – have a nucleolus, nucleus and cell wall. **Three-fold but One Cell**.
- ◆ **Matter** – which is spirit materialized, has a gas, liquid and vapor form. **Three forms but still matter**.
- ◆ **Triangle – has three equal sides (A=B, B=C, A=C).** The triangle shows the equal balance between the Father, Word and Holy Spirit – **they agree as One.**

Your understanding **WILL BE** illuminated beyond your imagination when you understand the construction and spiritual operation of the tabernacle pattern (Most Holy Place, Holy Place and Court Round About). **Luke 11:52** talks about a key that was lost. **THIS PATTERN IS THE KEY of UNDERSTANDING!** For more information about this divine pattern and other overlooked Biblical truths from both the Old and New Testaments, please visit http://www.idmr.net.

SETTING THE STAGE

In all referenced scripture passages where the names Lord, God and Jesus Christ are mentioned, this writer has chosen to insert the original Hebrew names: Yahweh (Lord), Elohim, which is plural (God) and Yahshua the Messiah (Jesus Christ). Historical records will show and prove the Hebrew name Yahshua was translated into Greek as Iesous and Latin as Iesus. Later Iesous was translated in the 16th century in the English language as Jesus Christ. The name of the Messiah, in Hebrew – his own language, is Yahshua, which means "Yahweh is salvation" or "Yahweh saves." The word "Christ" was originally a title rather than a proper name. The word "Christ" comes from Greek and means the anointed. In Hebrew the word is translated as Messiah.

If the seeker of truth **(DO YOUR OWN INVESTIGATION)** does a minor investigation of the English alphabet letters "Y," "I" and "J," one will find that the letter "J" was derived from the letter "I," and the letter "I" was derived from the letter "Y." A closer examination will prove that the letter "J" or sound of letter **"J" DIDN'T EXIST THEN, AND DOESN'T EXIST NOW**, in the Hebrew, Greek or Latin language.

Here is more evidence to consider. The below image is a bronze plaque that faces the west wall of Independence Hall (Philadelphia, PA, USA) beneath the portico archway. Notice the date–1778. Notice how "June" is spelled with the alphabet letter "I". This is because the alphabet letter "J" did not exist in our alphabet system at that time. To confirm the authentic nature of this image, please call the Independence National Historical Park Library and Archives at (215) 597-0060 or (215) 597-8047.

After careful consideration, it is easier to accept and use the original Hebrew names. We can understand, now, that "Jesus" would not have been the name that Miriam (Mary) was told by the angel Gabriel to give her "new-born" son **(Luke 1:21)**. As a Hebrew child growing up in Nazareth, the Messiah walked the earth plane some 1,500 years before the alphabet "J" was added to our English alphabet system.

Even the act of breathing – inhaling and exhaling – conforms to the two-syllable name Yahweh. "Everybody breathes, no matter what your nationality, and when you breathe you say "Yahweh." You can't breathe "Jehovah," "Allah" or "God." Everything was created to reflect him. To know the name of Yahweh is to know the divine attributes and the relationship of Yahweh to his people.

I'd like to thank Dr. Henry Clifford Kinley, who died in 1976, for sharing the divine panoramic vision and revelation he received June 6, 1931. Prior to receiving this divine vision and revelation, Dr. Kinley was an assistant minister of Church of God for 15 years. This vision and revelation completely changed the way he taught and preached and showed him how Yahweh would reconcile all denominations and world religions with the understanding and application of the

- Universal name of the creator – Yahweh, Yahweh Elohim and Yahshua the Messiah (**Ephesians 3:15**).
- Operation of the Divine Yahweh given Pattern.
- Correlation of the physical body to the Mosaic tabernacle and Solomon Temple (**1 Corinthians 6:19-20**).

Dr. Kinley founded the Institute of Divine Metaphysical Research (IDMR) with international headquarters in Los Angeles and 160 branch schools throughout the USA and other foreign countries. IDMR is not a church but a nonprofit, nondenominational religious and scientific research organization dedicated to showing proof of the existence of Yahweh and his eternal purpose, pattern and plan of salvation. The institute strives to bring to light the pervasive errors in doctrines of religious denominations to remove the vail of our carnality so that we may be quickened with the Holy spirit. We can not be getting ready, we must already be in the (kingdom) body of Yahshua the Messiah at the closing of this present (spiritual) age. Come out of darkness before it is too late and **Inherit Eternal Life Now!**

Free, open-to-the public lectures are provided to people of any denomination. None of IDMR ministers are paid for teaching the true gospel.

APPENDIX 1

 ## THE SIGNIFICANCE OF A GOOD EDUCATION

The Bible clearly tells us that knowledge, wisdom and understanding are distinct components of our intellectual make-up. **Proverbs 4:5** says, "Get wisdom, get understanding!" David had understanding, and David said in **Psalm 119:105**, "Your word is a lamp to my feet and a light for my path."

Acts 17:11 says, "Now the Bereans (scholars of that day) were of noble character than the Thessalonians, for they received the message with great eagerness and examined the Scriptures every day." **2 Timothy 2:15** says "Do your best to present yourself to Yahweh as one approved, a workman who does not need to be ashamed and who correctly handles the word of truth."

We need wisdom to understand the events that are unfolding around us in this chaotic and sinful world. The only weapon the unrighteous spirit (Lucifer or Satan the Devil) can effectively use against us is ignorance of spiritual truth. According to **Daniel 12:10,** "Those who are wise shall understand."

Speaking through the prophet Hosea, ELOHIM says in Hosea 4:6, "My people are destroyed for lack of (true and spiritual) knowledge. Because you have rejected knowledge." Scripture proves it!

- ◆ Knowledge without understanding is potentially dangerous.
- ◆ Understanding without wisdom is greatly limited.

To obtain Biblical and spiritual knowledge, you can read the advice given in **James 1:5.**

Ask for help in using your mind. **James 1:5 says,** "If any of you lacks wisdom, he should ask Elohim, who gives generously to all without finding fault, and it will be given to him."

Even King Solomon, the wisest man who ever lived, admitted to Elohim in **1 Kings 3:7**, "But I am only a little child and do not know how to carry out my duties." Remember to make wisdom (the application of knowledge) your goal and not just knowledge itself … a secret King Solomon learned.

Do you ask for wisdom? Yahshua the Messiah does not want us to grope in ignorance, which prevents salvation for our souls. In **1 Timothy 2:3-4,** he said, "wants all men to be saved and to come to a knowledge of the truth." **1 Thessalonians 5:21** encourages us to study the Bible to find truth but be careful to prove all things. Don't just assume that what you have always heard and believed is the TRUTH!

This is why **Romans 15:4** says, "For everything that was written in the past was written to teach us, so that through endurance and the encouragement of the Scriptures we might have hope."

Elohim in **2 Peter 1:2** says, "Grace and peace be yours in abundance through the knowledge (creator's purpose, pattern and plan) of Elohim and of Yahshua the Messiah."

IN THE FINAL ANALYSIS

In **Proverbs 3:13,** King Solomon said, "Blessed is the man who finds wisdom, the man who gains understanding."

King Solomon also said in **Proverbs 13:20**: "He who walks with the wise grows wise, but a companion of fools suffers harm."

Proverbs 15:33 says, "The fear of Yahweh teaches a man wisdom, and humility comes before honor." Learning to fear him and depart from evil requires that we study the scriptures to learn what to do. As we learn, we should be afraid to disobey what we have learned.

This is what Yahweh says in **Jeremiah 9:23-24:** "Let not the wise man boast of his wisdom or the strong man boast of his strength or the rich man boast of his riches, but let him who boasts, boast about this: that he understands and knows me, that I am Yahweh, who exercises kindness, justice and righteousness on earth, for in these I delight," declares Yahweh.

Here is the ultimate result of wisdom. **Daniel 12:3** says, "Those who are wise will shine like the brightness of the heavens, and those who lead many to righteousness, like the stars forever and ever."

In comparison to walking across the stage and receiving your graduation diploma or certificate, the spiritual reward is to be a recipient of the Holy Spirit that takes shape and form in your heart and mind. **Ephesians 6:11-18** words are soothing to the soul. "Put on the full armor of Elohim so that you can take your stand against the devil's schemes. For our struggle is not against flesh and blood, but against the rulers, against the authorities, against the powers of this dark world and against the spiritual forces of evil in the heavenly realms. Therefore put on the full armor of Elohim, so that when the days of evil comes, you may be able to stand your ground, and after you have done everything to stand. Stand firm then, with the belt of truth buckled around your waist, with the breastplate of righteousness in place, and with your feet fitted with the readiness that comes from the gospel of peace. In addition to all this, take up the shield of faith, with which you can extinguish all the flaming arrows of the evil one. Take the helmet of salvation and the sword of the Spirit, which is the word of Elohim."

My desire for you is stated by Paul the Apostle in **Colossians 1:9-10**: It says, "We have not stopped praying for you and asking Yahweh to fill you with the knowledge of his will through all wisdom and understanding. And we pray this in order that you may live a life worthy of Yahweh and may please him in every way: bearing fruit in every good work, growing in the knowledge of Yahweh." Stay alert and be ready!

APPENDIX 2

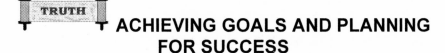 ## ACHIEVING GOALS AND PLANNING
FOR SUCCESS

Could some of us be making the mistake of looking to personal achievement and economic status as the ultimate benchmarks of success in life? Whether we describe it as the rat race or fast track or just the price of success, are we pursuing this journey with a spiritual eye?

The Bible never implies that it is wrong to achieve economic success or to be well known in our communities. It does not downgrade hard work and the desire to succeed, but rather talks about an attitude of mind. It is wrong to make worldly marks our primary goals in life. It is wrong to manipulate or hurt others or practice unethical maneuvers in striving to get ahead. It is wrong to covet power and prestige.

Our heavenly Father doesn't demand success but obedience from us. **Hebrews 11** gives us a list of people Yahweh considered successful. Some were rich, some were healthy, others were sick to despair. Some lived to advanced ages while many died early and sometimes violently. These people were all men and women of faith whose success was measured by higher spiritual standards. Each was obedient and each had the attitude of a servant.

Let's consider the Biblical example of Moses in **Exodus 3**. Do you remember what happened when Elohim spoke to Moses out of the burning bush and commissioned him to return to Egypt and tell Pharaoh to free the Israelites held in bondage? Moses responded with a list of obstacles he felt were too great. I'm not eloquent. I have a speech impediment. No one will listen to me. No one will believe Elohim has spoken to me. But Elohim would not let him say no. With his help, Moses became Israel's greatest leader.

Someone who is truly successful seeks to encourage, help and build up others. He or she is diligent in work, obedient and strives daily to live the right way. **Unity,** the thread of unity, that wonderful quality that **holds us TOGETHER in hard times** and **brings us JOY in good times** binds us to a common purpose and permits us to recognize our individuality. As David said in **Psalm 133:1**, "How good and pleasant it is when brothers **LIVE TOGETHER IN UNITY!**"

Seek Elohim's will concerning the goals you have established. **Psalm 127:1** says, "Unless Yahweh builds the house, its builders labor in vain." Our efforts are to be in accordance with His will for our lives. If they are in sync, He will bless and prosper them far above what we could accomplish by ourselves.

I realize this formula for success may be completely at odds with the values of our society. It goes against the teachings of today's popular short-cut books. Nevertheless, it is the basis for real and lasting success in our heavenly Father's eyes. This real success can be summed up like this: It is better to be **"WELL DOING" than "DOING WELL"** – the only real success.

Remember, **don't just set goals — set the right goals**. **Matthew 6:33-34** reminds us of this important point. It says, **"But seek ye first his kingdom (NOT YOURSELF FIRST) and his righteousness, and all these things will be given to you.** Therefore do not worry about tomorrow, for tomorrow will worry about itself. Each day has enough trouble of its own." Give your spiritual life top priority. Notice what Yahshua the Messiah promised, "If we maintain the right priorities, all these things will be added unto you." He who puts Yahweh first will be happy at last.

Feed on His spiritual word. Too many times we search the Bible for scriptures to satisfy our selfish wants and needs instead of searching the scriptures to learn more about our creator.

APPENDIX 3

THE SKY'S THE LIMIT PERSONALITY

The scriptures reveal a form of positive thinking that is different and infinitely superior to anything humans have conceived. The Apostle Paul in **Philippians 4:13** gives us the source we must consciously go to for help when we need to change our lives. This is the statement he confidently uttered more positively than any statement ever made by today's experts in the field of self-help motivation: "I can do all things through the Messiah who strengthens me."

In John 5:30, Yahshua himself declared, "By myself I can do nothing. I judge only as I hear, and my judgement is just, for I seek not to please myself but Him who sent me." Simply put, Yahshua did not preach a philosophy of the self-centered.

Even in **Jeremiah 10:23**, the prophet Jeremiah stated "that a man's life is not his own; it is not for man to direct his steps." Jeremiah did not say man cannot dream of steps to take and then take them by himself. Of course we can. We can do marvelous things, especially if we exercise our spiritual muscle, take the initiative, do our part and believe we can.

But what this really means is that it does not come from anyone's own self; rather, it should be placed with Elohim, who is able to properly and wisely direct such abilities. He will give direction and transform the self in every human — if we will allow it.

SIMPLY PUT, if you rely on "thinking big," all you will ever be is a big thinker. "Thinking big" or "thinking positive," by itself, cannot work. A person doing it Elohim's way can use his or her talents and can tap the benefits of positive thinking.

I'd like to share two Biblical examples with you. One deals with a winning attitude, and the other deals with thinking big. There is a lesson to be learned from these passages in **Joshua and Genesis**. The power of positive thinking must be used with certain guidelines.

For example, Joshua and Caleb were part of a team of 12 spies who went to scope out the promised land prior to the Israelites' journey. Only these two had a winning attitude and came back with a good report, a willing heart and huge clusters of grapes. The other 10 returned with an evil report and influenced the rest of the Israelites to rebel against Yahweh. Their doubting and disobedience grieved Yahweh and caused him to delay their entry into the promised land for 40 years.

For example, early in the history of mankind, people worked together to build a very tall tower that would reach up to what they imagined was heaven. Yahweh didn't intervene to stop all work on the project. He didn't deny what they set out to do and what they accomplished. **Genesis 11:6** says, "They have begun to do this, then nothing they plan to do will be impossible for them."

This incident shows that it may bring results, but it may not mean it is necessarily appropriate and good. They built the Tower of Babel because they did not believe that Yahweh would keep his promise to not destroy the world again by water. **Psalm 89:34** states, "I will not violate my covenant or alter what my lips have uttered." In **2 Peter 3:9** it is stated, "Yahweh is not slow in keeping his promise, as some understand slowness. He is patient with you, not wanting anyone to perish, but everyone to come to repentance." Consider this – when it rains a rainbow appears. Yahweh established this covenant to remind His people that he would not destroy the world again with water.

Yahshua stated in **Luke 18:14** that "For everyone who exalts himself will be humbled, and he who humbles himself will be exalted." Frequent expressions such as self-assertiveness, self-confidence, self-fulfillment and a positive self-image promote self-idolization. There is nothing wrong with improving the self, but you have to be conscious about placing self before and above spiritual principles.

APPENDIX 4

TRUTH **PERSONAL AND CAREER DEVELOPMENT**

Personal and Career development evolves and blossoms over time. Self-leadership is giving direction and control to one's own actions. It is the most fundamental type of leadership. The Bible tells us in **Proverbs 25:28**, "Like a city whose walls are broken down is a man who lacks self-control." This passage shows us that being able to govern oneself is just as important as outward accomplishments.

Patience, self-control and due diligence is certainly required to reach your full potential. **Psalm 32:8** provides us with simple guidance. "I will instruct you and teach you in the way you should go; I will counsel you and watch over you." **1 Peter 5:6-7** says, "Humble yourselves, therefore, under Yahweh's mighty hand, that he may lift you up in due time. Cast all your anxiety on Him because he cares for you." Yahweh, not man, sanctions your steps and pathway.

When we think of Him, who He is, what He did for us, and what He offers us, we have to say, "How can we do anything less than worship Him in spirit and in truth?" **Romans 12:1-3** says, "Therefore, I urge you, brothers, in view of Yahweh's mercy, to offer your bodies as living sacrifices, holy and pleasing to Yahweh – this is your spiritual act of worship. Do not conform any longer to the pattern of this world, but be transformed by the renewing of your mind. Then you will be able to test and approve what Yahweh's will is – his good, pleasing and perfect will. For by the grace given me I say to every one of you: Do not think of yourself more highly than you ought, but rather think of yourself with sober judgment, in accordance with the measure of faith Yahweh has given you."

Listen to the fruit of your conversations. Are they eliminating problems or enlarging them? Are they conveying valuable knowledge or worthless gossip? **1 Thessalonians 5:11** says, "Encourage one another and build up each other." Ask your heavenly Father to bless your conversations with others and help you become more aware of what you say or how it may impact others.

If you hold up your head with a smile on your face and are thankful, you are truly blessed because the majority can, but most do not. Live your faith and live what you believe. Keep smiling inwardly and outwardly as you develop into an individual with character, recognizing it is not your position but your disposition that defines who you are. In **Samuel 16:7**, we are reminded of this one simple truth – "Yahweh does not look at the things man looks at. Man looks at the outward appearance; but Yahweh looks at the heart." A word to the wise...don't get caught up in your vanity and egotistical mindset.

Instead, **Make Your Blessings Count!** The gifts our Heavenly Father has given us are the gifts to enrich the lives of others. The harder you work at what you should be, the less you'll try to hide what you are. Remember to live your life in such a way, that those who know you, but don't know Yahweh, will come to know Yahweh, the creator of all life.

APPENDIX 5

KEEP YOUR INTEREST AS WIDE AS YOUR MARKETING OPTIONS

The Bible sets before us two ways of life, asks us to examine our beliefs and tells us in **Deuteronomy 30:19-20** that we should choose right over wrong. In this physical existence, we have only two options. One is the righteous path; the other is the unrighteous path. **Romans 9:21** asks the question, "Does not the potter have the right to make out of the same lump of clay some pottery for noble purposes and some for common use?" Either you are a vessel of honor or a vessel of dishonor.

The story in **Exodus 32:25-28** will help explain the point of being on the right side. The event takes place after Moses comes down from atop Mt. Sinai and sees the children of Israel worshiping a golden calf – an idolatrous image. His anger waxes hot, and he stands in the gate of the camp and says, "Who is on Yahweh's side? Let him come unto me." The Levi tribe (who was in charge of the Mosaic tabernacle and its upkeep) gathered those on Yahweh's side together as they went through the camp. Three thousand men, who were not on the right side, fell by the sword that day. **WHICH SIDE ARE YOU ON … the righteous or unrighteous path?**

Everywhere you look, there is a different church denomination on every corner of every street. Many people are running to and from these churches searching to find the truth and never, ever learning the truth. As a result, there are thousands of denominations or doctrines with different beliefs, theories, concepts and opinions. Each claims and professes their way is the truth. With this said, it is obvious many erroneous doctrines are leading the masses astray. **1 Corinthians 1:10** says, "That all of you agree with one another so that there may be no divisions among you and that you may be perfectly united in mind and thought." The truth is expressed in **John 15:16**. It says, "You did not chose me, but I chose you." There is only one way. Yahshua said in **John 14:6,** "I am the way and the truth and the life."

Luke 12:32 says, "Do not be afraid, little flock, for your Father has been pleased to give you the kingdom." **Colossians 1:13-14** says, "For he has rescued us from the dominion of darkness and brought us into the kingdom of the Son he loves, in whom we have redemption, the forgiveness of sins." The definition of Kingdom is found in **Romans 14:17**, telling us, "For the kingdom of Yahweh is not a matter of eating and drinking, but of righteousness, and peace and joy in the Holy Spirit." And **Matthew 13:47-49** says, "The kingdom of heaven is like a net that was let down into the lake and caught all kinds of fish." It further goes to say, "When it was full, the fisherman pulled it up on the shore. Then they sat down add collected the good fish in baskets, but threw the bad away. This is how it will be at the end of the age. The angels will come down and separate the wicked from the righteous."

My desire is that Yahshua the Messiah be more perfectly confirmed within each of us and that He becomes a conscious and effectual part of our everyday life. It's more than quoting scriptures, singing in the choir, or participating in some worshipping service. It's about our walk, our interaction with others and how we live our life. Let us be mindful and be more like Paul, who stated in **Ephesians 3:1** that he was taken captive against his own will with the end result of becoming that "righteous vessel unto honor."

APPENDIX 6

TIME POWER – THE ART OF GETTING AHEAD

THE PERFECT TIME IS ELOHIM'S TIME. HE is always in the present. HOW? HE INHABITS ETERNITY **(Isaiah 57:15)**, and within eternity there is no element of time.

Elohim's clock is never slow, but ours is often fast. Man watches the clock and always thinks about the past, present and the future.

Isaiah 64:4: Time spent waiting on Elohim is time never wasted. Our heavenly Father "acts on behalf of those who wait for him." Elohim challenges us to live for eternal values in the midst of a world that is rapidly passing away.

1 John 5:14 reminds us, "If we ask anything according to His will, he hears us."

In **Galatians 4:4-7,** Apostle Paul said that when the fullness of time came, Elohim sent his Son to redeem those in the world. There is a fullness of time for everyone. But we often want to hurry. When we rush HIS timing, we are like children who want to see what a rose looks like and force open the bud – killing the rose. Yet if we let our life unfold in its own time, in our heavenly Father's plan and purpose, it will be beautiful. In His time, HE will turn every adversity into victory.

WE OFTEN FIND IT DIFFICULT TO WAIT ON ELOHIM AND LET HIM SOLVE OUR PROBLEMS.

Is this because we have become accustomed to immediate results? For example, we live in the age of instant. Our fast-moving world demands immediate service.

Think about this: We microwave meals, get quick cash from automated teller machines, electronically file income taxes to get faster refunds, carry portable telephones for instant connectivity, go to one-hour film development and one-hour eye glass places. The list is endless. If stores don't provide instant service, we take our business elsewhere.

The demand for fast action or instant relief also spills into the spiritual realm. When trouble comes and our lives begin to unravel, we expect to solve the problem with a hasty prayer and a few insincere resolutions. The Psalmist David wanted release from his distresses **(Psalm 25:17),** and he prayed, "My hope is in you all day long." **(Psalm 25:5)**. In **Psalm 27:14**, David said, "Wait for Yahweh, be strong and take heart and wait for Yahweh."

The application of this one principle will relieve stress from so many lives. It is simply patience. Exactly what is patience? To quickly summarize, patience is "strength harnessed; power focused and faith taking its time." Why not put some patience in your life!

Lastly, **Proverbs 27:1** states it bluntly – "Do not boast about tomorrow, for you do not know what a day may bring forth." The only preparation for tomorrow is the right use of today.

I've often heard and sincerely believe that tomorrow is the barred and bolted door that has shut many people out of heaven. Take time today to find out more about our Creator, his purpose, pattern and plan. Why continue to wait? A spiritual alignment will add balance in your life and will bring peace, joy, and happiness to your soul. Meditate on the spiritual principals and precepts to experience the awesome power on a continual basis.

APPENDIX 7

 **PLAN TODAY OR PAY TOMORROW**

We live in a topsy-turvy world of confused money values. In an age of unprecedented prosperity and opportunities, our generation needs moral and spiritual guidelines about wealth and material possessions. Biblical warnings are not against prosperity or making a just profit, but rather against greed and selfishness.

What is True Success? Can it be measured in terms of a bank account? What does True Happiness consist of? Is it Money? Is it Power? Is it Fame? We need to be careful not to confuse mere material wealth with success or happiness. Possession of material riches without inner peace is detrimental to your soul. Instead, we need to view success and happiness the way our heavenly Father does. When we begin to see life the way our heavenly Father intends, we spend our efforts serving others, enabling others, seeking to make them happy — recognizing that happiness is not a result of accumulating material wealth. And that is when we find happiness and success.

What about your relationship to money? **Luke 12:21** says, "This is how it will be with anyone who stores up things for himself but is not rich toward Elohim." Are you seeking to be **RICH in GOODS** or **RICH in ELOHIM**? **2 Corinthians 4:18** so eloquently says, "So we fix our eyes not on what is seen, but on what is seen. For what is seen is temporary, but what is unseen is eternal"

Do we use it wisely, or does it control us? **Mark 8:36** says, "For good is it for a man to gain the whole world, yet forfeit his soul?"

Is money your servant or your master? According to Yahshua in **Matthew 4:10 and 6:24**, "We cannot serve both Him and money. Money is a good servant, but a cruel master. If money is your highest goal, the thing you long to gain, its power will enslave your soul and cause your life much pain. People who misuse and abuse the power of money are simply poor people with money."

CAUSES OF THE LOVE OF MONEY – NEVER SATISFIED

Those who seek riches and wealth will never be satisfied. King Solomon pointed out this tendency in **Ecclesiastes 5:10-11:** "Whoever loves money never has money enough; whoever loves wealth is never satisfied with his income. This too is meaningless."

As the Apostle Paul put it in **1Timothy 6:10**, "For the love of money is a root of all kinds of evil." It is not so much what we do with money – it's because of what it can do to us. It corrupts the human spirit.

In **Luke 12:15,** Yahshua often warned about the potential corrupting influence of riches. "Then he said to them, Watch out! Be on your guard against all kinds of greed; a man's life does not consist in the abundance of his possessions."

These verses are directed to the rich who see themselves as self-reliant, trusting in their wealth with no need for spiritual guidance and no compassion for others. Consider the disastrous effect wealth had on King Solomon. He had lavish wealth, but it helped to ruin him spiritually because he did not use it properly. If this greed happened to a man of such great wisdom, it could certainly happen to you and me.

Yahshua in Mark 10:24-25 echoes these same words, "Children, how hard it is to enter the kingdom of Yahweh! It is easier for a camel to go through the eye of a needle than for a rich man to enter the kingdom of Yahweh."

James 4:2-3 says, "You want something but don't get it. You kill and covet, but you cannot have what you want. You quarrel and fight. You do not have, because you do not ask Yahweh. When you ask, you do not receive, because you ask with wrong motives, that you may spend what you get on your pleasures."

THIS IS THE ANSWER...

In our materialistic world, we would do well to heed these words of caution about the dangers of unrestricted wealth. Our heavenly Father knows that we attach great importance to the physical and this interferes with our spiritual values – the basis for happiness.

In contrast to the "greed" or "never satisfied" attitude is the example of Job, a man of wealth and of confidence in Elohim. Elohim allowed the devil (who falsely accused Job) to take Job's possessions, children and health **(Job Chapters 1-2).** The devil took the view that the rich express confidence in Elohim only so long as He prospers them. In the end of the account, Elohim blessed Job with twice as much as he had before **(verse 10)**.

Riches do not buy one's way into the spiritual kingdom. But the rich, who see their mortality, humble themselves, submit to his righteous spirit and become "rich in good deeds, and to be generous and willing to share." **(1 Timothy 6: 18).**

Yahshua counseled a course of action that contradicts the common practice of amassing ever greater amounts of wealth. He advised people to look to Yahweh – the source of all wealth. These same words are echoed in **Matthew 6:33**, "But seek first His kingdom and his righteousness, and all these things will be given to you as well."

Yahshua told his followers in **Matthew 6:19-21**, "Do not store up for yourselves treasures on earth, where moth and rust destroy, and where thieves break in and steal. But store up for yourselves treasure in heaven, where moth and rust do not destroy, and where thieves do not break in and steal. For where your treasure is, there your heart will be also." He wanted his followers to have their minds fixed on the internal treasure – the spiritual kingdom. Storing spiritual treasures is far more important than being physically prosperous. Anything physical is expendable. **1 Timothy 6:7** says, "For we brought nothing into the world, and we take nothing out of it."

So don't allow the desire for riches and great wealth to become your chief desire or let it become a consuming passion. This will help prevent falling into the miserable trap that has ensnared so many – being a victim of get-rich-quick schemes or practices of unethical financial endeavors. A burning desire for more possessions, more money, better cars, better homes, better clothing and a more glamorous life-style has robbed people of many of the *real values* of life – profitable friendships, a happy marriage, happy children and the joy of serving others. The apostle Paul in **1 Timothy 6:17** warned that we should not "put our hope in wealth, which is so uncertain, but to put our hope in Yahweh, who richly provides us with everything for our enjoyment."

117

Thank Him and seek His wisdom if you have been blessed with wealth. **James 1:17** states it eloquently, "Every good and perfect gift is from above, coming down from the Father of the heavenly lights, who does not change like shifting shadows." These are unmerited gifts - blessings that belong to Elohim and come from him. We didn't do anything to earn them. The blessings that really count are spiritual blessings that cannot necessarily be physically seen but can be perceived by faith **(Hebrews 11:1-2)**.

He wants us to prosper in all things and be in good health. In **John 10:10**, the Messiah says, "I have come that they may have life, and have it to the full**." Ecclesiastes 5:18** states, "It is good and proper for a man to eat and drink, and to find satisfaction in his toilsome labor under the sun during the few days of life Yahweh has given him – for this is his lot."

REMEMBER THIS. "A man reaps what he sows" says **Galatians 6:7**. In more modern terms, "What goes around, comes around."

APPENDIX 8

 **It's Your Future. Plan and Create It.**

DID YOU KNOW – Those who fear the future will likely fumble the present? Stated another way – you cannot change the past, but you can ruin the present, worrying about the future. Don't be afraid to trust an unknown future to an **ALL-KNOWING** Elohim!

Hebrews the 11th chapter talks about faith and provides an excellent example and road map to follow. In many passages it talks about patriarchs who demonstrated faith. For example, **Hebrews 11:8** says, "By faith Abraham, when called to go to a place he would later receive as his inheritance, obeyed and went, even though he did not know where he was going." You can't easily answer all of life's questions. You must have faith! Try not to let your fear of the unknown keep you from making spiritual progress. We must not be afraid to take that leap of faith. We can overcome uncertainty by trusting Elohim. He sees beyond the unknown.

Simply remember – the *TASK AHEAD of YOU* **is never as great as the** *POWER WITHIN YOU!* Stated differently, our endurance is not of ourselves, but of the Holy Spirit in us.

YES, we don't know what's ahead and what the future holds. But Elohim does. He can help you avoid pitfalls and troubles by giving you the wisdom you need, when you need it. If you are using some limitation or hardship as an excuse for falling short of Elohim's best, it is time to change your attitude. Each day we encounter situations and challenges that cause us to become weary and discouraged. Wherever we are, whatever bold endeavor we are involved in for Him, or whatever battle we may fight with our spiritual enemy, we have the confidence that Yahweh is with us.

Perhaps right now, as you read this book, you are struggling with decisions that will impact you and your lifestyle: whether to continue college because of financial hardships, whether to propose or accept a proposal for marriage, whether to start a business of your own, whether to move to another state or to another country for that dream job or even alter your basic beliefs.

2 Corinthians 4:7 states, "We have this treasure in jars of clay to show that this all-surpassing power is from Yahweh and not from us." **ACTS 17:28** simplifies it even more. It says, For in him we live and move and have our being." We are complete with Him in us. Without a doubt, HE is the light that surrounds us; HE is the love that enfolds us; HE is the power that protects us. His presence watches over us and where we are, that is where HE is.

Consider this food for thought ... no matter which way you turn or look...

Looking Back...   He is our Creator (Colossians 1:16).
Looking Ahead...   He is our Judge (2 Corinthians 5:10).
Looking Up...   He is our Savior (Philippians 2:5-10).
Looking Down...   He is our Sustainer (Colossians 1:17).

Looking Right... He is our Teacher and Comforter (Matthew 23:8 and John 4:24).

Looking Left... He is our Advocate (1 John 2:1).

Looking Within... He is our Life (Galatians 2:20 and Colossians 1:26).

FACE THE FUTURE WITH CONFIDENCE

To enjoy the future, accept our heavenly Father's forgiveness for the past and follow the advice of one of the greatest texts in the Bible – **Philippians 3:13-14,** which tells us, "Forgetting what is behind and staining toward what is ahead, I press on toward the goal to win the prize called me heavenward in Yahshua the Messiah." That is our job – to accept his invitation for salvation and to go forward with our lives in obedience, never looking back with longing. This is the crowning achievement for any individual when he begins to spiritually walk in the "newness of life," focused on Yahweh's purpose, pattern and plan.

Even **Ecclesiastes 9:10** warns us to make the most of life now while we have the opportunity. "Whatever your hand finds to do, do it with a all your might, for in the grave, where you are going, there is neither working, nor planning nor knowledge nor wisdom."

Hebrews 12:1 tells us, "Let us run with perseverance the race marked out for us." Good runners look ahead, concentrating on the finish line and beyond. **Luke 9:62** says, "No one who puts his hand to the plow and looks back is fit for the service in the kingdom of Yahweh."

YOU ARE A WINNER

You can feel confident that your spiritual future is as bright as the promises of Elohim. Your endeavors will succeed with Yahweh at the helm. Yahweh does not ask about our ability or inability, but only about our availability, and if we prove our dependability, Yahweh will take care of our capability. Yahweh does not demand success from us, but obedience to HIS will.

Give thanks for your answered prayers by proceeding without any doubt. Have faith in your abilities. Feed your faith, and doubt will starve away.

John 16:13 – He guides us into the truth.
Romans 8:26 – He helps us pray and is the only intercessor (not any man); we are his children.
Ephesians 3:16 – He strengthens us with power through His spirit.
2 Corinthians 3:18 – He transforms us into His spiritual kingdom and His image.

1 John 2:25: "And this is what he promised us, even eternal life." His offer is not a gamble but a guarantee. **John 17:3** tells us eternal life is predicated on knowing your creator as He is and actually exists. **DO YOU KNOW HIM** in a personal way? The thought that troubles me is that people put more hope in winning big in a sweepstakes or lottery than they do in gaining eternal life.

2 Timothy 1:7 reminds us, "For Yahweh did not give us a spirit of timidity, but a spirit of power, of love and of self-discipline." *Lastly...2* **Corinthians 5:7** sums it up perfectly, "We live by faith, not by sight". In your journey, embrace mental thoughts and demonstrate actions that show you are "led by the spirit" because you "walk by the spirit."

Below are several scriptures that will build your faith:

Ephesians 2:10: "For we are Hs workmanship, created in Yahshua the Messiah unto good works, which Yahweh prepared in advance for us to do."

Psalm 55:22 tells us, "Cast your cares on Yahweh, and he will sustain you; he will never let the righteous fall."

Proverbs 3:5-6 promises: "Trust in Yahweh with all your heart and lean not on your own understanding; in all your ways acknowledge Him, and He will make your paths straight."

Isaiah 54:17: "No weapon forged against you will prevail, and you will refute every tongue that accuses you."

Psalm 84:11: "For Yahweh is a sum and shielded; Yahweh bestows favor and honor, no good thing does he withhold from those whose walk is blameless."

1 Peter 1:9-10: "For you are receiving the goal of your faith, the salvation of your souls. Concerning this salvation, the prophets, who spoke of the grace that was to come to you, searched intently and with the greatest care, trying to find out the time and circumstances to which the Spirit of Messiah in them was pointing when he predicted the suffering of Messiah and the glories that would follow. It was revealed to them that they were serving themselves but you, when they spoke of the things that have now been told you by those who have preached the gospel to you by the Holy Spirit sent from heaven. Even angels long to look into these things."

Psalm 89:34: "I will not violate my covenant or alter what my lips have uttered." Consider this – a rainbow appears when it rains. Yahweh established this covenant to remind His people that he would not destroy the world again with water.

Romans 13:11 says, "And do this, understanding the present time. The hour has come for you to wake up from your slumber, because our salvation is nearer now than when we first believed." The night is nearly over; the day is almost here. So let us put aside the deeds of darkness and put on the armor of light. Let us behave decently, as in the daytime, not in orgies

123

and drunkenness, not in sexual immorality an debauchery, not in dissension and jealousy. Rather, clothe yourselves with Yahshua the Messiah, and do not think about how to gratify the desires of the sinful nature."

Begin each day with a prayer that asks for protection and guidance against evil thoughts and actions of your own and others.

✱ ✱ ✱ ✱ **Resources** ✱ ✱ ✱ ✱

Think and Grow Rich – A Black Choice
Dennis Kimbro, Ballantine Books, 1991

Power Thoughts
Michael Kelly, Kelly Enterprises, 1997

The Success System That Never Fails
W. Clement Stone, Prentice Hall, 1962; Pocket, 1980

The Seeds of Greatness
Dennis Waitley, Pocket Publishing, 1984

It Only Takes A Minute To Change Your Life
Willie Jolly, St. Martin's Press, 1997

Powerbase: How To Build It, How To Keep It
Marilyn Moates Kennedy, MacMillan Publishing Company, 1984

Maximize Your Potential
Arthur L. Andrews, 1994

Power of Purpose
Robert Allen, Berrett – Koehler, 1997

Black Enterprise Magazine – The Publisher's Page
Earl G. Graves, Black Enterprise, 2002

Success Strategies
Adele Scheele, Harper Trade, 1987

Getting Through To People
Jesse Nirenberg, Prentice Hall, 1974

See You At The Top
Zig Zigler, Pelican Publishing, 1984

Elohim, The Archtype (Original) Pattern of the Universe
Dr. Henry Clifford Kinley, Institute of Divine Metaphysical Research, 1961

Thank You for purchasing my book. 20% of the proceeds from all book sales will go to the Inspire Me Scholarship for minority students.

For more information about Harlynn LaVance Hammonds and his mission to uplift the human spirit with **inspirational plaques and empowerment T-shirts**, please visit his web site at www.xpressionsoftheheart.com or call at 1-800-633-5883.

Aspiring Authors: Our publishing division – Inspire Me Publishing, can help take your typed manuscript to print and to market.

Harness Your Potential to Enrich the World

For **business automation tools and internet marketing solutions** from Harlynn LaVance Hammonds, please visit the companion web site at www.onenumbersolution.com or call 1-800-633-5883.

OneNumberSolution.com

"Giving Your Business the Unified Advantage"

INDEX

ABOUT THE AUTHOR

Harlynn LaVance Hammonds is a man on a mission with a message to kindle a positive epidemic in your work and your life. He shares practical and personal insights from lessons learned through life experiences, observations and hard knocks. He has 17 years experience in leadership - management positions in the computer and telecommunications industry and is a licensed minister. LaVance Hammonds is the recipient of many awards in the military and professional arena such as the Public Affairs Officer of the Year and the National Alliance of Business Industry Cluster Award. He has published articles on time management, career development and black history contributions in the military. His entrepreneurial direction with

"Xpressions of the Heart", "Inspire Me Publishing" and "One Number Solution" is focused on enabling others to become and live their vision. His seminars have inspired others to look within, reach out and move ahead in their lives. He lives near Washington DC, and is a graduate of Grambling State University, a historically black college.

Invite Harlynn LaVance Hammonds to speak at your next meeting, conference or special event. Phone (800) 633-5883.

Printed in the United States
18569LVS00006B/322-357